THE SHROUD OF CHRIST

By PAUL VIGNON D.Sc (Fr)

TRANSLATED FROM THE FRENCH

WITH NINE PHOTOGRAVURE AND COLLOTYPE PLATES AND
THIRTY-EIGHT ILLUSTRATIONS IN THE TEXT

THE BOOK TREE
SAN DIEGO, CALIFORNIA

Originally published 1902
E.P. Dutton & Co.
New York

New material, revisions and cover
©2002
The Book Tree
All rights reserved

ISBN 1-885395-96-5

Cover layout and design
Lee Berube

Printed on Acid-Free Paper
in the United States and United Kingdom
by LightningSource, Inc.

Published by
The Book Tree
P O Box 16476
San Diego, CA 92176

We provide fascinating and educational products to help awaken the public to new ideas and
information that would not be available otherwise.
Call 1 (800) 700-8733 for our *FREE BOOK TREE CATALOG*.

FOREWARD

Over the years many books have appeared about the Shroud of Turin, the possible burial cloth of Christ. Jesus is said to have been buried while wrapped in this cloth, which may account for the mysterious "burned-in" image of a man exhibiting the same wounds Christ is believed to have had as a result of his crucifixion.

Some speculate that the image results from a chemical reaction that took place at the moment Jesus rose from the dead. People's bodies don't normally re-animate themselves, but it is believed that such a thing, when and if it should occur, would result from a completely natural but unknown phenomenon. According to this book, it is this phenomenon that is responsible for the markings on the shroud, and it puts forth evidence to support this theory.

This was the book that revealed the Shroud of Turin "negative image" photographs —it was the one that broke the story to the world, so great scientific care was given to support the potential legitimacy of the shroud. Therefore, this work should not be left out of print and forgotten. It is time to present it again to the world, offering one the ability to relive the discovery and study information that might otherwise be lost in support of (and possibly against) the shroud being a legitimate and genuine relic from Christ.

Is this an actual "photograph" of Jesus printed by chemical reaction? Later books on the subject, at least some of them, have come out as the "final word" on the subject, proclaiming that the shroud has clearly been proven as a medieval fraud based on Carbon-14 dating. Other books soon followed, escalating the argument by showing how this "proof" cannot be completely verified or accepted. The debate still rages, so it is time to return to the first book on the subject—this one—which seems to have been forgotten amidst all the confusion.

After over a century of debate and exploration into this subject, there are those who are convinced that they know the final answer—people from both sides of the argument. Pure reason, with no room for the slightest degree of faith, tends to discredit the evidence in support of the shroud. A certain amount of faith, however, brings one into line with believing that enough evidence exists to accept the shroud as genuine.

It all depends on how one looks at the matter. Proof seems to exist in favor of both sides, which complicates the situation. Therefore, it would be helpful to return to the first, definitive book on the subject, despite its bias, and examine it closely. One who opposes should look for holes and flaws, while those in favor should study the supporting evidence.

The Shroud of Christ tells exactly how the original "negative image" discovery was made, which is the most important facet of this enduring mystery. This book is without a doubt the essential introduction to the Shroud of Turin mystery.

Despite the fact that Carbon-14 dating has been done on the shroud, we have since found that this scientific test is not and can not provide the final proof to the shroud's authenticity. The tests seemed to show that the shroud dated to sometime in the Middle Ages, yet some claim that this data could be flawed because the shroud was involved in a fire at about the same time, which could have affected the results. With Carbon-14 tests being inconclusive, at least in this case, science has so far failed to win its battle with religion. Despite those incessant debunkers who claim that everything has a rational answer, the world will always have its mysteries. This remains one of them.

We do not know with complete certainty if the shroud is genuine. At the same time, science has failed to prove *without any doubt*, with absolute, unquestionable proof, that the shroud is a fraud or fabrication. As with all miracles (if indeed this is one), the question must always remain open. Due to this fact, we must remain open to the possibility that the shroud is truly genuine—a miraculous and mysterious relic that could offer us an interesting kind of "proof" that relates to Jesus, the power of God, and our own human souls. We must learn more in these areas in order to recognize such "proof", should it exist, but being open to it is something that should not be entirely discounted in light of the information presented in this incredibly interesting book.

If one is open to the possibility of miracles, or that there are laws or powers that we are still unable to explain, then this book should be studied closely. It can also prove valuable to those who remain skeptical on the matter, due to its immense amount of original information that can be studied or researched further.

Paul Tice

CONTENTS

THE HOLY SHROUD

From the painting by Giulio Clovio (16ᵗʰ century).

PLATES

ILLUSTRATIONS IN THE TEXT

ILLUSTRATIONS IN THE TEXT

INTRODUCTION

O N May 1, 1898, an exhibition of sacred art was opened at Turin, and the Government of His Majesty King Humbert authorized the public display of a very precious relic, which had belonged to the Royal House of Savoy since the middle of the fifteenth century. This relic (a large piece of linen cloth) was kept rolled up within a metal casket, secured by many locks, and was said to be the Shroud of Christ. The casket might only be opened with the Royal permission, and by consent of the Archbishop. The piece of cloth had only been previously displayed to the public six times during the nineteenth century. In 1814 by Victor Emmanuel I; in 1815 at the request of Pope Pius VII; in 1822 upon the accession of Charles Felix; in 1842 and in 1868 at the marriages of Victor Emmanuel I and of Prince Humbert. When the exhibition of 1898 took place no one had seen it for thirty years.

This piece of linen cloth had been known historically in the East since the year 1353. It had been handed down by its successive owners as having been the actual Shroud of Christ, used when the disciples took down the body from the Cross. The brown stains visible on it were said to be the actual impressions left by the body. Careful inspection shows that these stains occur upon the cloth in such a fashion as to represent two bodies, lying head to head, the one seen from the back, the other from the front.

Our frontispiece is a reproduction of a painting by Giulio Clovio, a well-known pupil of Raphäel; this painting, preserved at the Royal Pinacothek of Turin, gives us both the general aspect of the cloth, and the way in which the body must have been laid upon it.

All through the Middle Ages, and in our own times as recently as 1898, those who accepted the authenticity of the Shroud believed, in a general way, that the stains were caused by liquid blood combined with aromatics (such as aloes), used *before* burial. This burial having been provisional and very hurried, the simple explanation arrived at was that the disciples had not been able to wash the corpse. It seemed, therefore, quite natural that the linen cloth should have stains on it, and that it should have retained the double impression of the body. The stains, which corresponded to the features of the face, seemed a mere superficial indication, such as might have been expected considering the roughness of the mechanical process in question.

As for the large class of those who, throughout all ages, have been incredulous about relics brought from the East after the Crusades, it seemed to them more likely that the impressions were merely painted, and had therefore no intrinsic value.

It was natural to think that the linen cloth had at first been used in religious rites as a simple accessory of ceremonial, gradually being raised to the dignity of a precious relic. We know the curious power of generation and unconscious growth which characterizes legends of this description.

As a matter of fact, since the beginning of the eighteenth century, historians, such as Baillot and Fleury, had known that a relic, said to be the Holy Shroud, but which no historic document authenticated, had been the subject of open controversy among ecclesiastical authorities. Two bishops had even given grounds for their opposition to its authenticity ; the summary of the letter written by the second of these bishops to the reigning Pope was known. It was also known that the Pope had issued a Bull, in which the Shroud was spoken of as simply a copy of the real Shroud of Christ.

A sequence of events, to be set forth hereafter, caused the relic to be transferred from Champagne to Savoy. There it secured powerful protection, and was once more recognized as authentic. Little by little, however, the traditional importance of the Holy Shroud lessened, except in Northern Italy and Savoy, where the formal exhibitions of relics at the time of the Renaissance and during the seventeenth century, were still held in remembrance. This Shroud, so long famous, had not, it is true, shared the sad fate of another so-called Holy Shroud, that of Besançon, which had equally claimed to be authentic. The Holy Shroud of Besançon

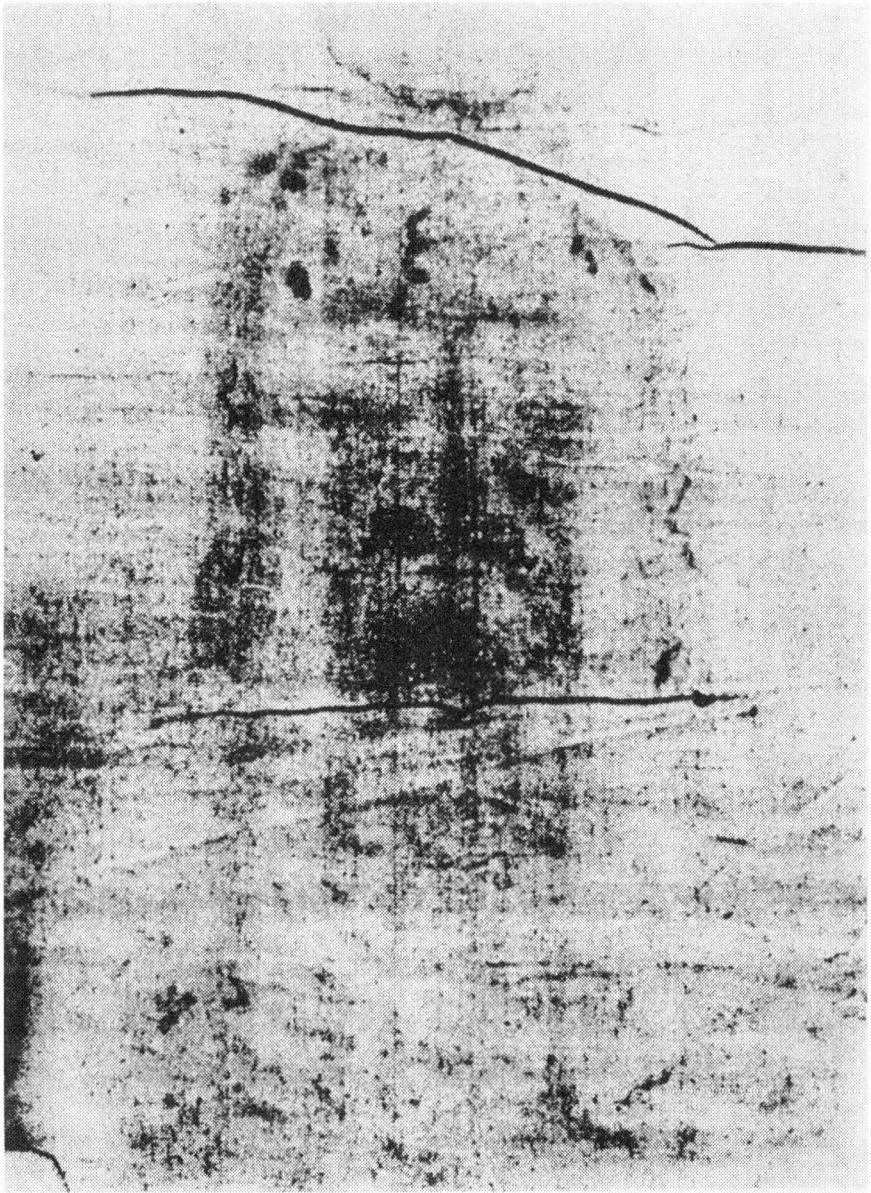

Heliog.Wahl Imp.Ch.Wittmann, Paris

THE HEAD
as seen on the Shroud

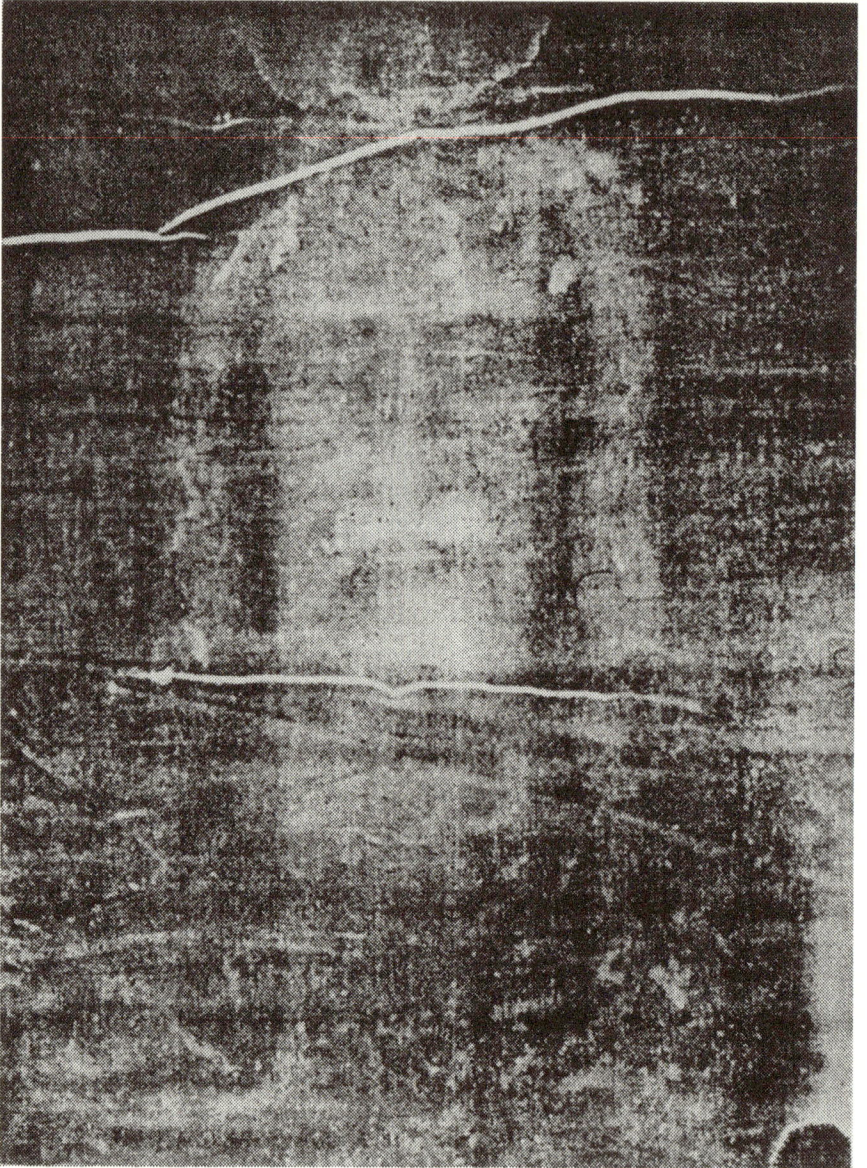

Héliog. Wahl

Imp. Ch. Wittmann, Paris

THE HEAD

as seen on the photographic negative plate

had been pronounced fraudulent, and the ecclesiastical authorities had given orders that it should be made into lint. The destruction which seemed to menace the Shroud of Turin was more gradual, but not less sure. Oblivion fell upon it, the rarity of its exhibition inducing the belief that precautions were taken to preserve under polemical shelter an object to which it was not desired to draw attention.

An unexpected change came in 1898, when the Holy Shroud was photographed and the result published to the world.

The markings on the Shroud were found to have the characteristics of a photographic negative, in that, on the photographic plate, which reverses the lights and shades, a positive portrait revealed itself. Those who examined this portrait pronounced it to be remarkable. They declared that no painter of the Middle Ages could have possibly produced so wonderful and perfect a picture, much less any kind of pictorial negative. In France a learned writer, M. Arthur Loth, Lauréat de l'Académie des Inscriptions, published a pamphlet drawing attention to these facts.

Was the Holy Shroud, so long ignored, about to acquire scientific fame ? Not at all. To those interested in the matter it seemed that darkness had definitely closed round the relic once more. As a matter of fact, the religious world received M. Loth's pamphlet with reserve, awaiting the decision of science. Experimental science however did not seem to perceive that a problem had arisen in the solution of which it had any definite interest.

Historians, on the other hand, were on the alert. They judged, and with reason, that this thing concerned them also.

They desired to sift to the bottom the history of the so-called relic in the far-off fourteenth century. The existence of the papal Bull was remembered. M. le Chanoine Chevalier, Correspondent de l'Institut, sought for and discovered the original letter which had provoked the papal Bull. In this letter there was an allusion (vague, it is true) to an avowal, said to have been made to a previous bishop by the forger himself. This seemed to close the discussion, and the president of the Académie des Inscriptions, at a solemn sitting held on November 15, 1901, whilst awarding a gold medal of 1,000 francs to M. le Chanoine Chevalier, did not hesitate to severely censure any future attempt to impose upon the credulity of the faithful with what could henceforth be described only as a fraudulent misrepresentation.

But, it may be asked, in this purely historical discussion, what was thought of the curious facts revealed by photography in 1898 ? Were they not as convincing as the somewhat obscure events of the fourteenth century ? Perhaps these physico-chemical facts might have kept the balance of the scales level, if they had not seemed to dissolve like a mirage at the first cold breath of critical inquiry. It was alleged that the opinion of a distinguished physicist had been sought by M. Chevalier, and although the exact terms of his opinion were not made public, it was believed to be definitely unfavourable. Indeed, if the impressions on the Shroud were of the nature of photographic negatives, it was impossible to believe them genuine, as no artist of the fourteenth century was acquainted with the methods of photography.

Although criticism was directed from all sides against what was called the "photographic evidence," it was sufficient only to glance at the original proofs to realize that here was grave matter for consideration.

The physicist to whom M. Chevalier had appealed, pronounced the pictures to be incontestable negatives as soon as he was able to examine the photographic proofs. The proofs, which had at first been looked at sceptically by scientific men, determined not to be influenced by traditions, were examined again with growing attention, and soon seemed worthy of minute study.

The results of this study, lasting over a year and a half, are what we place to-day before the public. They appeal not only to archaeologists and students in the laboratory, but also to the world of Art, and to those who are interested in facts which bear on the foundations of our modern society.

Our researches have been carried on without prejudice, and with equal respect to the claims of conflicting beliefs.

In order to approach the subject with the calmness of academic discussion, we shall avoid as long as possible all mention of the historic personage to whom these pages refer. From the moment that it becomes

INTRODUCTION

inevitable for science (in order to explain the marks left by a corpse on the Shroud at Turin), to inquire into the special circumstances attending the death of the man whose body was enveloped therein, we shall call upon documentary evidence to furnish us with certain indispensable particulars. In consulting these documents, we shall lay stress only on those facts which every one must consider to be historically proved.

The Shroud at Turin, however interesting scientifically, remains a nameless shroud unless we can definitely establish that it must have been the Shroud of Christ.

We therefore eliminate all that may have been said or thought by man, in the course of centuries, about the origin of this relic. For us it is simply a large piece of linen cloth, four metres ten centimetres in length, one metre forty centimetres in width ; discoloured by time ; worn and torn in places ; half burnt by fire—bearing upon its surface shadowy impressions, just as it appears on Plate IV.

I have to thank those who have furnished me with certain technical particulars. Especially I should like to express my gratitude to M. le Professeur Yves Delage, Member of the " Académie des Sciences," and M. le Dr. E. Herovard, " *Maître de Conférences* at the Sorbonne." Without their constant support and counsel it would have been impossible for me to finish the task which they encouraged me to undertake.

I have asked M. le Baron A. Manno and M. le Chevalier Pia to accept my dedication of this book. M. Manno was president of the Exhibition of 1898 ; he directed the photographic work, by means of which men of science can to-day investigate a problem of absorbing interest. M. Pia is the artist, who is so highly thought of in Italy, and whose photographic work is so remarkable. The Official Commission of 1898, seeking for some one whose scientific loyalty equalled his ability, could not fail to ask his co-operation. He has taken the trouble to prepare the plates for me, from which the engravings have been executed, for the illustration of this work. I must also make special mention of the assistance which has been given me by M. le Commandant Colson, Professor of Physics at the " École Polytechnique." He was peculiarly fitted by his previous work to deal with the problems involved.

CHAPTER I

GENERAL DESCRIPTION AND EXAMINATION OF THE IMPRESSIONS VISIBLE ON THE HOLY SHROUD—THE APPEARANCE AND SIGNIFICATION OF THE MARKS

GENERAL DESCRIPTION AND EXAMINATION OF THE IMPRESSIONS VISIBLE
ON THE HOLY SHROUD

A T first sight the stains on the Shroud form an extremely confused whole. Some of them seem to converge along the centre of the linen cloth ; these are of a reddish brown colour. Others are distributed in parallel groups, just outside the reddish marks. These are blackish in tone. At first it would seem a difficult task to disentangle these markings, but as we discern that the brown stains along the centre are the marks of the back and front surfaces of a man's body, and that the blackish marks are the traces of fire, we shall begin to interpret rightly the impressions on the Shroud. To do this we must dismiss from our minds the various erroneous interpretations which have been brought forward from time to time by persons who had not the photographic proofs before them. The ground will then be comparatively clear.

Gradually we shall find that the impressions yield up their secrets. The realm of the unknown will narrow with each step gained. Plain, simple observation will prove to us that the impressions are not the work of a painter, but that they are the actual marks, left by a human body on the linen cloth—marks produced long ago by some action, other than direct contact, set up between that dead body and the linen cloth.

The impressions date historically from so far back that they can only have been the result of some spontaneous phenomenon. No one in the Middle Ages had the knowledge necessary for their production by handicraft.

We do not yet know how the marks were made, any more than we can tell the name of the man whom the linen cloth enshrouded. But these two problems are not insoluble, and we shall deal with them further on. A list of recent publications referring to the Holy Shroud will be found at the end of the volume.

THE APPEARANCE AND SIGNIFICATION OF THE MARKS

The upper part of the plate which we have selected for reproduction as our frontispiece, shows us a large piece of linen cloth which angels are unfolding and offering. That is the Holy Shroud. The painter, Giulio Clovio, a pupil of Raphäel, has given the shadowy marks quite simply; the general effect is that of two bodies—one seen from the back, the other from the front—lying head to head at the centre, with the feet at either end of the cloth.

We have reproduced the general aspect of the Holy Shroud on Plate iv. It is a facsimile of the photographic print obtained by M. Pia. The exigencies of space compel us to give the linen cloth as though cut in half, the front view of the body and the back view of the body are thus shown side by side instead of head to head, as in the original. Let us examine them each in turn.

As soon as we begin to distinguish the front aspect of the body, what strikes us most is the truly singular modelling of the head. Plate ii. gives it us less reduced. Certainly this is not a beautiful head. It is very difficult even to make out the features. There is the nose, but it seems quite black. As for the eyes, they seem to be hidden by spectacles, or to be encircled by a white rim. We can say that there is a mouth, but we cannot really see it. Which is the upper lip? Where is the lower lip? We cannot tell. The face, thus strangely modelled, is no less strange in its general shape, which is that of a rectangle. Of ears or neck there is no trace. On each side two dark bands seem to represent the hair. Below the face they terminate abruptly. Doubtless the hair fell behind on the shoulders. But where are the shoulders?

Let us, however, pursue our investigations. Downwards from the head the impression becomes gradually more strongly marked, until it is interrupted by a wide band of lighter colour. The deepest tone corresponds to the breasts; the light band represents the depression beneath

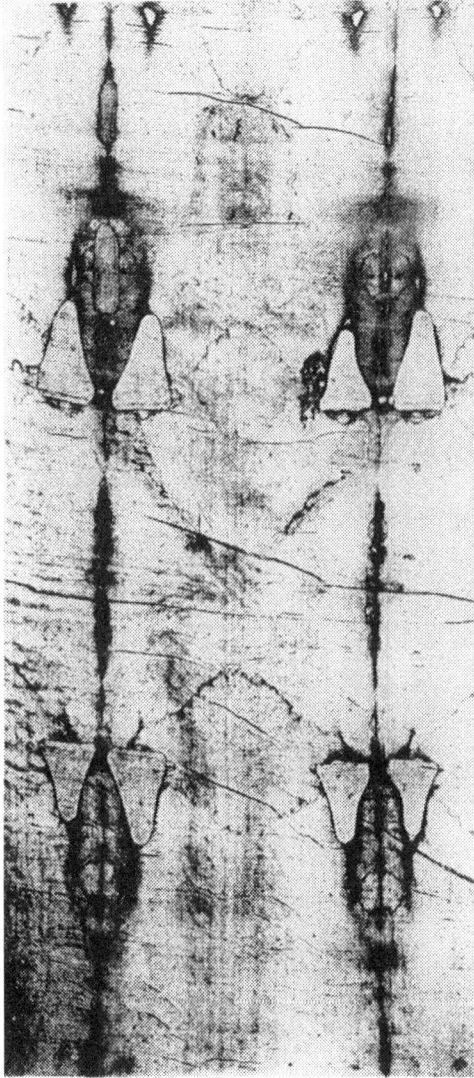

Heliog Wahl

Imp. Ch Wittmann, P

Upper half
showing front view
of the figure

FACSIMILE OF THE SHROUD

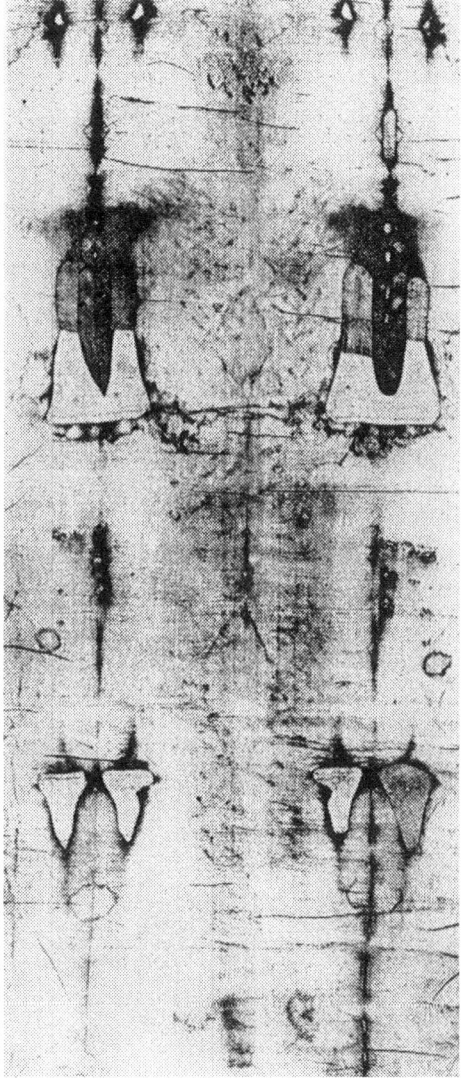

Lower half
showing back view
of the figure

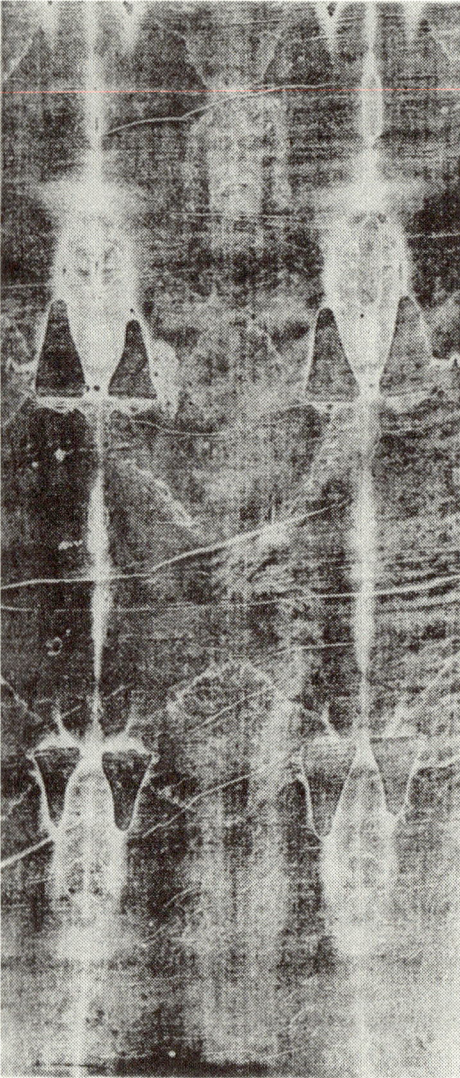

Heliog Wahl

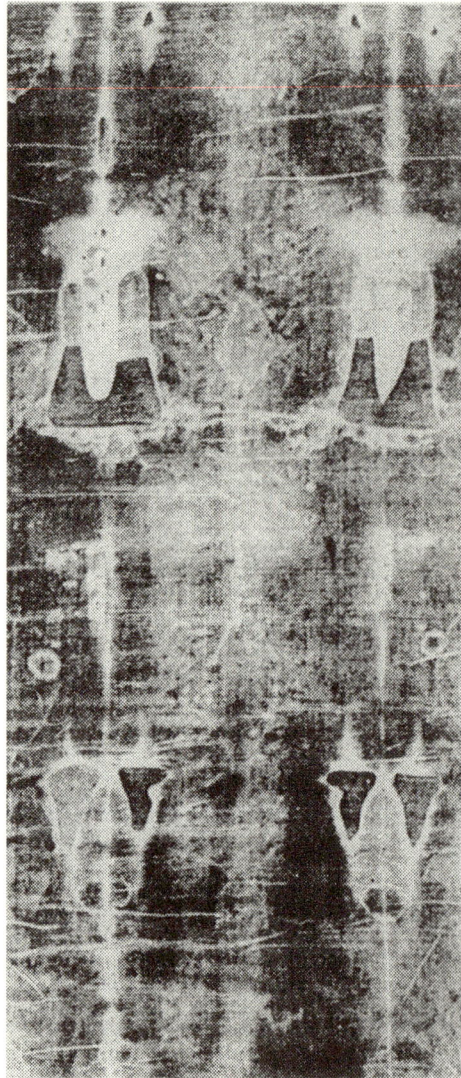

Imp. Ch. Wittmann, Paris

THE HOLY SHROUD

Facsimile of the Photographic negative plate

them. Lower down, a vague smudge, shadowy at the borders, marks the position of the stomach. Left and right of the abdomen are the fore-arms : we can distinguish one hand, doubtless folded over the other hand, of which only the fingers are visible, and we can perceive that the pelvis widens out in normal fashion ; here are the thighs, one hardly perceptible, the other reduced to a narrow strip. The figure seems cut off at what, to judge from the distance from the knee, should be the ankles. The ankles themselves are not to be seen. Instead comes a dark strip, much wider than it need have been, and fainter in tone towards the edges. In noting the details of this print, we asked ourselves whether on the actual linen cloth the feet were visible in the front view. M. le Baron A. Manno was very willing to enlighten us on this point. As a matter of fact, the cloth is longer than the photograph represents. But at the Turin Exhibition they had been obliged to fold under the two ends of the cloth, in order to shorten it. The Official Commission had had a great oblong case prepared, in which the relic was to be placed on the altar in the chapel, called " The Chapel of the Holy Shroud." No one had seen the linen cloth since 1868, and thus an error was made in the requisite dimensions of the case, which proved to be considerably too short. This regrettable mistake was not discovered until it was too late to rectify it. No one then dreamt that this display of the relic would lead to a scientific study of it. No one had yet thought of photographing the Shroud, therefore the case was used just as it was, both the ends of the cloth folded under. That is why in this plate we cannot see the feet. We shall get further details on this point from certain other plates later on.

Let us now examine the back view of the figure, shown on the right of Plate IV.

Here we see the back of the head. The shoulders, a little too high, are very distinct. Lower down, two dark patches, one specially marked, represent the shoulder blades. Beneath them the sweep of the back is broadly indicated, the impression growing fainter at the sides, and fainter also towards the loins.

At this point the picture is intersected by marks which converge towards the centre of the material. Lower down the position of the more fleshy portions is clearly discernible ; lower still the hollow space is shown where the thighs separate. All the parts near the thighs are only vaguely indicated ; lower again we come to some transverse folds in the linen cloth, level with which there is a lessening in tone which would correspond to the hollows behind the knees. Lower still it is just possible to see the calves of the legs, and a very faint zone of shadow, hardly visible on one side, corresponds to the tendons of the heels. The heels themselves are perfectly visible ; and part of the soles of the feet, but there was no space for the great toes on this plate.

It is a very delicate matter to deal with these prints. The reader should look at the plates from a little way off, comparing them with the reproductions on Plate v.

The reproductions have not all been equally successful, because, above all things, we desired that there should be no touching up.

So far we have not mentioned the dark brown stains to be seen on many parts of the body. These stains are clots of blood. We will not take them into account until we seek to identify the man whose body has left these traces on the Shroud.

However extraordinary it may seem that the two surfaces of a human body should be found thus marked on the Shroud, there is no ground for supposing that they were drawn, stained, or painted by man. A glance shows us how difficult it would have been for an artist to produce such an effect by pictorial work. Moreover, the result could never have satisfied those who might have instigated such extraordinary work. Every one who has seen M. Pia's photographs has come to this conclusion.

Another solution immediately occurs to our minds. The marks have a strange resemblance to impressions left on the cloth by a human body. The most prominent parts are those which are best reproduced. The less prominent parts and the hollows are less visible or not visible at all.

Before going further let us try to interpret the meaning of the dark patches, which constitute so large a part in the markings on the cloth, and which even hide the upper part of the arms in both pictures.

The blackish marks on the cloth are perfectly symmetrical in their distribution ; so are the marks which stand out upon them distinctly like white footprints. The black markings are places where the cloth has been burnt ; the white marks are places where the stuff has been actually burnt through and afterwards patched with some white material. There are twelve blackish marks, of which we see only eight on Plate IV. The other four were on the ends of the cloth, which, as we said, were folded back for want of space in 1898. All twelve may be seen on our frontispiece (Giulio Clovio's painting).

It is well known that the Royal Chapel, where the relic was kept, was partially destroyed by fire in 1532. When this misfortune happened the Shroud must have been folded as we should fold a cloth before putting it away in a cupboard ; that is to say, folded in half down the centre and again in half lengthways, then folded across several times. The fire consumed one corner of this folded bundle ; therefore, when the cloth came to be unfolded, there were as many marks of burning as there had been folds.

These are not the only traces left by the fire which so nearly destroyed the Holy Shroud. There are also to be seen lozenge-shaped marks, of a yellowish colour, surrounded by jagged lines, rather darker. These also are at regular intervals on the cloth, level with the burns.

In the front view of the figure, one of these lozenge marks comes on the lower part of the chest ; the next is level with the knees. In the back view a small one comes just below the shoulder blades ; one rather longer is over the thighs. A large stain covers the space where the two heads meet. Besides these lozenge marks, which occur along the centre of the cloth, there are half lozenges which occur at the sides, parallel with the others.

These yellowish stains are easily accounted for. When the cloth was rescued from the fire it was drenched with water, without time being taken even to unfold it. The Shroud dried badly, and one of the corners of the bundle remained wet. The stain thus produced was in the shape of a right-angle triangle; four of these angles when unfolded produce the lozenge-shaped marks down the centre of the cloth ; the half lozenges are where the cloth was in two folds, not four. If we fold a piece of paper in four, and tear off the fourfold corner, the hole so made will be lozenge-shaped, just like our yellowish stains. On the Shroud, the part which remained wet corresponds to our torn angle of paper.

The only other traces of the fire still to be dealt with, are the water stains across the region of the loins, seen from the back. Here a trickle of water highly charged with burnt particles must have run along the middle fold of the cloth, thus making a long stain on both surfaces. This is probably the origin of the dark line which cuts the figure just above the loins, and which has been mistaken by many people, for the marks of the chain which bound our Lord to the scourging post.

At first it may seem grievous that the Holy Shroud should have come down to us so sadly dilapidated, but we shall find that all the marks and stains will help us in our study. It is easy to see that the two figures on the Holy Shroud are the front and back aspects of a man's body. What relation do the figures bear to one another ?

The first glance shows us that if the marks are actual impressions— that is to say, if the linen cloth really enshrouded a human body and *retained the marks thereof*—then the figures are disposed in a perfectly legitimate manner. If we were to place a man's body upon one half of a long piece of cloth, draw the cloth over the head and cover the front of the body with the other half of the cloth ; if we could then employ some process by which the modelling of the body could be printed off on the cloth, we should have two figures, the top of the two heads being the point of junction. At this point the two figures would merge together, and so long as the cloth remained on the body, the marks of the back and front portions would correspond to one another, the breasts being marked opposite the shoulder blades, the gastric region level with the loins, the knees opposite the hollow behind the knees. If the body were removed and the cloth opened out, we should have the double imprint just as if we had opened out a double mould, the two impressions lying on the cloth head to head, and corresponding symmetrically to one another.

It is so evident that the figures are the front and back halves of a double impression that every one who is inclined to believe that the effect was wrought pictorially must at least admit that the artist has tried to give the effect of a body having been so enshrouded.

20

APPEARANCE AND SIGNIFICATION OF THE MARKS

Those who have seen the marks on the Holy Shroud have long considered them to be actual impressions. In this respect no description would help us so much as does the object lesson given us by Giulio Clovio in our frontispiece. In the foreground of his painting is stretched the body of Christ, the feet together, the hands crossed, just as they are in Plate IV.

Giulio Clovio has made one slight error in depicting the right hand as crossed over the left. It should have been the left over the right. On the cloth, certainly, the right hand appears to be uppermost, just as the wound mark on the cloth seems to be on the left side instead of the right ; the rights and lefts being reversed as they would be in a double mould.[1]

Joseph of Arimathea and Nicodemus, aided by St. John, are just about to lay the cloth carefully over the body, the Holy women helping them. Giulio Clovio shows this being done at the foot of the Cross—not at the sepulchre—an artistic licence which we will gladly excuse, since it gives us the unity of place. In the distance, on the opposite hill, we get a glimpse of Jerusalem. The unity of time is obtained by an even bolder licence. Above the Cross, among the clouds, three angels extend the Holy Shroud with the double impression already on it. Other little heads are painted among the clouds ; angels hurrying to see the precious winding sheet of Christ. But that is not all ; not only are the impressions completed in heaven, at the same moment that on earth Christ is enveloped in the Shroud, but the cloth already bears the traces of the fire in 1532 ! Let us admire this last mark of artistic conscientiousness, for it proves to us that the painter had before him this very cloth, the photographs of which we are studying to-day.

The problem before us is this : Are the marks on the Holy Shroud actual impressions, or are they simply an ingenious fraud ? Our opponents pronounce them fraudulent, and say that the forger has betrayed himself by leaving a space between the two heads, whereas they should have been joined together.

M. de Mély is one of these, and we quote his own words : " M. Loth

---

[1] We lay stress upon this slight mistake of Clovio's simply to show how difficult it would be for an artist not to betray himself by some similar slight error of detail.

should not have omitted to explain to us why there is a gap between the two heads when, if the Shroud had been really wrapped round the corpse, the outline of the head would have been one solid block shaped like a cylinder instead of two ovals."—*Chronique des Arts et de la Curiosité, Supplement to the Gazette des Beaux Arts*, September 8, 1900, p. 304.

This objection is easily disposed of. If a body were covered with a cloth as in the picture by Giulio Clovio, the cloth would have to be adjusted behind the head with the most minute exactness, or there would be a space between the two ovals of the head. This is just what must have happened, from the very fact that Joseph of Arimathea and Nicodemus are each holding an end of the upper part of the cloth, stretching it between them.

In the actual Shroud the outline of the heads is not so sharp as it is in Giulio Clovio's picture.

We get a better idea of it from Plate IV., where it is impossible to say where the front and back impressions join each other. This extreme vagueness of outline is one of the essential points to be accounted for, and we may mention here some observations which we made with reference to some mummies brought from Egypt by M. Gayet (*Journal des Débats*, June, 1902). M. Gayet showed them lying with small rolls of linen placed at the sides of the head to support it, and beneath the chin to keep the mouth shut. Often there were also rolls of linen on the top of the head, which made a kind of bandage. The rolls of linen at the sides of the head were fairly thick, like small cushions, filling up the space between the head and the shoulders. Such rolls as these would fully account for the peculiarities we notice on the Shroud, where the gradual lessening of the reddish tone, which represents the top of each head, shows that the cloth has gradually lost contact with the hair, and, as we know, the ears and neck are not visible.

We are now familiar with the general aspect of our piece of linen cloth. Is it worth all the trouble which we have taken, and which we ask our readers to take ?

If we confine ourselves to the study of Plate IV. or of Plate II., on which we see the head alone, reproduced on a larger scale, we must admit that the impressions are not attractive. Giulio Clovio himself has not succeeded in making them so. Extended like a sign-board in the middle of his exquisite painting, the Holy Shroud looks both fantastic and incomprehensible.

But if we look for a moment at Plate v., or better still at Plate iii., we shall be convinced that the outlines visible on the Shroud are worthy of the deepest attention. The Shroud is a mysterious enigma, only to be read with a magic key. Since 1898 the key is ours. Photographic apparatus and a sensitive plate have revealed to us, by inversion, the true solution.

On such a plate the whites of the cloth become black, and the browns and blacks white.

The half tones all take their exact relative values. For example, on the Shroud the nose is a dark shadow lighter at the edges. On the photographic plate it is light in the centre and a little darker at the sides, where the nose joins the cheeks ; again, on the Shroud the eyes are dark spots circled with white ; on the photographic plate they regain their normal aspect, and stand out in delicate relief. We know that objects are thus reversed in photography. This fact is too well known to need emphasis. The photographic plates, therefore, which reproduce the negatives on the Shroud, interpret all the strange spots and stains, showing us plainly the figure of a man. The outlines are so blurred that we get the effect of seeing him through gauze, or in semi-darkness. First we distinguish the head, proud and energetic ; then less distinctly the different parts of the body. If we look steadfastly, everything will gradually explain itself, and even certain distortions which puzzle us, will be accounted for by degrees.

The modelling of the figures becomes positive on a negative photographic plate, but it is just the opposite with all the other marks which we noticed on the Shroud.

We have said that certain dark brown stains were marks of blood ; they stand out quite distinctly against the half tones of the body. On the photographic plate these dark spots are of course, as nearly white, as they were before nearly black.

That is not all ; the blackish marks of fire stand out nearly white against the linen background, which in its turn has become black ; the white patches of material with which the cloth was repaired are now almost black. The water stains are inverted too. They now look lighter, instead of darker than the surrounding cloth.

Thus neither on the positive Plates II. and IV., nor on the negative Plates III. and V. are the impressions perfectly rendered.

Briefly let us summarize these first observations. The marks visible on the Holy Shroud of Turin may be compared to a photographic negative in so far as the general modelling of the body is concerned. This is proved because the negative photographs of this negative give that same modelling in positive. The wounds, on the contrary, are represented in *positive* on the Holy Shroud.

Naturally, the burnt marks, the patches used in the mending, and the stains of water, etc., are all visible on the Shroud as they actually exist ; it could not be otherwise.

One thing more. When we study M. Pia's photographs or their reproductions, how can we be sure whether we are looking at the Shroud as it actually is, or at the photographic rendering of it, which reverses all its values ? We know in this way : The photograph of the Shroud as it actually is, will give the burnt marks black, and the patches used to repair the burns, white, just as they are in the actual Shroud itself. Another way would be to examine the various copies which from time to time have been made of the Holy Shroud. Plate IX., for instance. Here all the values are given exactly as in Plate IV., which proves that Plate IV. represents the material as seen by the naked eye.

Our readers may say that all this is so obvious that any one could have discovered it. No doubt it was open to every one to arrive at our conclusions, but had they done so, we should not now have to reply to the many objections which have been raised, and which we propose to deal with further on. Our whole argument hangs upon whether we are able to prove that the Impressions on the Shroud have been spontaneously produced, and that they are *not* the work of man.

CHAPTER II

THE REASONS WHICH CAUSE US TO ATTRIBUTE THE IMPRESSIONS ON THE HOLY SHROUD TO THE BODY OF JESUS CHRIST

WE will now try to establish, from the evidence of the Shroud itself, the identity of the man whose body left these impressions. The time has come to approach the question from this new point of view ; not merely for the satisfaction of what must be considered legitimate curiosity, but because it is necessary, for the complete achievement of the task we have undertaken, to know every circumstance that can be ascertained, relating to the death and enshroudment of the historic personage whose identity is in question.

The traditions already existing with regard to the Shroud made us think of experimenting as to the chemical properties of aloes and of febrile sweat. The results of our experiments fulfilled our hopes, and we shall describe them in our last chapter; but we must now call upon the Shroud itself to tell us whether our hypothesis led us in the right direction.

We first thought of making experiments as to the properties of aloes, because it was possible that we were dealing with the impression left by the body of Christ. We will not conclude that the body *was* actually that of Christ, simply because our chemical experiments have succeeded.

THE WOUND-MARKS OF CHRIST

The wound-marks upon the body, as seen in the Holy Shroud, are so special in their character that they point at once to the body of Jesus Christ.

THE SHROUD OF CHRIST

All round the head, on the forehead and among the hair, stand out distinct brown stains which look like clots of blood. These stains form a crown. We are reminded at once of the Crown of Thorns.

On the right side of the breast is a lentil-shaped patch, four to five centimetres in length. Just below this are other marks, which would seem to be the stains of flowing blood ; flowing, that is to say, while the body was in an upright posture.

Once more we remember that " one of the soldiers with a spear pierced His side." Doubtless if the mark to which we have called attention is indeed a stab from a lance or a spear, such a wound would have caused death, unless indeed the sufferer were already dead when he received it, for if the blow had been in an oblique direction from right to left, it must certainly have pierced the heart ; and even if this were not so, the quantity of blood-stains show that some of the main blood-vessels of the body must have been severed.

On the left wrist is a brown mark which must also be from a clot of blood. The right wrist is not visible, but both the forearms bear distinct traces of flowing blood. It would seem almost certain that this man had received wounds in the wrists, and that the blood streaming therefrom, and coagulating, had left the traces which we see. These marks again recall to our mind the wounds made in our Saviour's body when He was nailed to the Cross.

At the heels and on the soles of the feet similar marks are visible. Is it not fair to claim that they correspond to the wounds made by the nails with which Christ's feet were pierced ? True, in the photographs of the front view of the body there are no traces of blood at the lower extremities, but the feet are almost entirely hidden, as already explained.

This is not all. On the back, on the fleshy parts in the vicinity of the pelvis, on the thighs, and even on the calves are a curious series of marks, almost alike in shape and regular in direction. We know that Christ was scourged on the very morning of His death, and the inevitable conclusion is that these marks were produced by some instrument like a scourge, and indicate not so much the strokes of a rod or of whipcord, as of the button-tippéd, knout-like instruments of flagellation used by the Romans.

Behind the right shoulder (the left as seen on the Shroud) is a large blotch, striated vertically, and extending from the crest of the shoulder bone, along the shoulder-blade. We know that Christ was "compelled to bear His Cross"; the Cross was so heavy that it could not but cut the flesh.

The face is evidently bruised. In describing its modelling we have already mentioned a disfiguring lump which breaks the line of the nose; we also noticed the swellings on the cheeks and cheekbones. It will be remembered, that the night that Jesus was taken prisoner and brought before Caiaphas, the high priest, His assailants spat in His face and buffeted Him. As St. Matthew relates in his twenty-sixth chapter, at verses 67, 68 : "Then did they spit in His face and buffeted Him; and others smote Him with the palms of their hands, saying, Prophesy unto us, thou Christ, Who is he that smote Thee?"

We have shown that this man had received at least *one* mortal wound. But the whole aspect of the features, as shown in the impression, is corpse-like. Notice how the nostrils are pinched, and how the calm of death spreads over the whole face. The passion of suffering is past, the peace of death is attained, the sacred sacrifice completed. "It is finished."

There can be no shadow of doubt that the body here enshrouded was that of one who had undergone the penalty of death. That the cloth we speak of, was veritably his shroud. More than all, that this body bears unmistakably the wounds which were inflicted on Christ, and the marks of the Cross on which He died.

Was this man in very truth—The Christ?

If the impression on the Shroud was, as we believe, spontaneously produced, and if this impression shows, as we think it does, so many remarkable and concordant characteristics, surely we have every right to conclude that the body was none other than that of Jesus Christ our Lord.

This conclusion cannot be considered as a mere hypothesis. We arrived at it inevitably by a series of direct observations. But in order to still further prove our argument, let us now ask, Would it have been conceivably possible to produce such wound-marks fraudulently upon the impression left by some other dead body ? Or, even if the impressions are altogether spontaneous, do the distinctive marks which we have pointed out prove necessarily that the body is that of Christ ?

EXAMINATION OF THE WOUND-MARKS ON THE SHROUD

We have only to look at the wound-marks to be able to say that they are not the work of a forger.

Let us suppose, for instance, that some man in the Middle Ages, an inhabitant, we will say, of Byzantium, or even the self-avowed forger himself, whose confession was published by the Bishop of Troyes, has before him a large piece of linen cloth, on which are already two impressions of a human body. He does not know how the impressions were made, but he sets himself to paint in the wound-marks ; he may even use blood instead of paint ; the impressions may now pass for those of Jesus Christ, no matter whose they were originally.

Is not this a perfectly natural hypothesis ?

No, because where could he have procured the linen cloth bearing such impressions ? But, granted that he *had* procured it, we say that he would not have *known* how to paint in the wound-marks, and that if he had *known* he would not have *wished* to represent them as they are in fact represented.

In the first place, the wounds are too real, too natural in all their details to be fraudulent. (We hope to show later on how forgers did set about their work.) For example, let us look carefully at the wound in the breast ; it has the aspect of a clot, formed by the blood which flowed from the wound, when it was inflicted—the flow of blood indeed is represented with perfect exactness. It would have been difficult for any painter to give so perfectly the curves and windings of a liquid, adapting itself to the inequalities of the surface which it encounters. Indeed, to give adequately the true appearance of a similar wound, the highest skill would have been necessary : it could not have been done by allowing blood, human or other, to trickle over the linen cloth, for, as we shall show, the linen has not here been in contact with flowing blood enough to wet it. When we pour blood upon

28

a dry cloth, or upon a cloth which has been soaked in oil, the fibre of the stuff absorbs the liquid by capillary action, so that it spreads unevenly along the threads, thus making stains with jagged edges. On the Shroud, the clot on the breast shows itself clearly outlined, *not* with jagged edges. We must therefore suppose that the forger used some method of painting. Now, as the stuff is lissome and pliable, it could not have retained any thick paint requiring body-colour; consequently our painter must have applied some sort of stain, with enormous skill, to give the required effect. This supposition we consider to be, if not absurd, at least unlikely.

Let us turn now to another wound, the reproduction of which would have required even greater ingenuity and skill. We allude to the large drop of blood visible on the forehead above the left eyebrow.

This drop springs from a definite point, indicated by its darker colour (see Plate ii.). This dark point corresponds to one of the wounds made by the crown of thorns. The blood which has flowed therefrom has met in its course the two wrinkles of the forehead, and has, by this slight opposition, been forced to spread itself out, forming two small horizontal pools ; thence it continued to flow, until it ended in a tear of blood close to the eyebrow, and having thus flowed, it dried upon the skin.

Now any drop of blood, drying thus, upon a substance into which it does not penetrate, takes, when coagulated, a sort of basin-like shape, a section of which we give here (Fig. 1). The border or brim of the basin is formed by the fibrine of the blood, containing the red corpuscles in its coagulum ; the centre is composed of the serum, which in drying takes a dull brown tint.

SECTION THROUGH A DROP OF BLOOD WHICH HAS DRIED ON AN IMPERMEABLE SUBSTANCE.
Fig. 1.

Here, as the liquid part of the serum evaporates, the convexity of the centre is depressed. The contour of the drop of blood preserves, however, the same shape as it had when it was fresh.

Now this description applies exactly to the blood-drop on the forehead. In the parts where the blood has flowed, and where it has accumulated in sufficient quantity, it is bordered by a dark edge. The centre of the little stream, and the centre also of the terminal tear, are of a lighter tint. This drop of blood is reproduced not only with the greatest minuteness and delicacy, but with entire faithfulness to scientific detail.

No painter, in his most elaborate work, has ever risen to such exactitude, as a glance at any of the numerous representations of Christ, Crowned with Thorns, will show us.

In most of such paintings, the artists have been quite neglectful of the wrinkles, or other obstacles, which a flow of blood would meet with in its course, and they have also painted such blood-streams, too narrow at their start, and too wide as they continue to flow : very often giving them symmetrical shapes, as in the Holy Face of Zeitblom, dating from the fifteenth century, which is in the Berlin Gallery.

Not only must we remark how, upon the Holy Shroud, the exact natural conditions of the coagulation of blood are reproduced, but also it is necessary to observe that if the figure on the Holy Shroud is indeed that of Christ, the blood which had flowed from the wounds made by the crown of thorns, would have been long dry when the entombment took place, at least ten hours later. It cannot have taken much longer than an hour for the blood on the face to coagulate. If, then, it had been found that the blood from the forehead had left its impression on the linen while still wet, it would have been possible to suspect a fraud ; but as we have found that the marks have been spontaneously produced from blood which was already *dried*, we can only conclude that Nature has set the seal of truth upon the Shroud.

By what laws, then, physical or chemical, have the clots of blood reproduced themselves upon the linen cloth ?

First of all, from a physical point of view, it would seem that the blood-marks make a direct positive impression upon the Shroud, exactly contrary to what we had observed regarding the other marks ; and this can be explained. The blood has acted very powerfully, and, as might have been expected, the edges of the clots, thick and prominent, have acted more strongly than the depressions in their centres. Moreover the linen is actually stained the same colour as the clots by contact with them, and is therefore also darker at the edges and less dark in the middle. That is why these marks are positive. The other brown marks on the Shroud correspond, as we know, to the light parts of the body itself. We shall touch on this subject again when we point out that the impressions on the Holy Shroud afford us no data from which to determine the true colour of the hair and beard.

From a chemical point of view the blood has re-acted on the cloth by the carbonate of soda and the urea which are found in the serum as well as in the sweat. M. Ganthier remarks in his *Chimie appliquée à la physiologie* (vol. i., p. 447) : "*La réaction alcaline constante du sang provient du bi-carbonate de soude et du phosphate tribasique de soude dissous dans son plasma. Cette alcalinité augmente dans le sérum après la formation du caillot*"; and in the same work (vol. ii. p. 315): "*L'urée augmente souvent dans le sang pathologique, spécialement dans les fièvres inflammatoires. De ces observations Picard conclut que dans le sang l'urée, augmente pendant les affections fébriles.*"

Our experimental researches, as to the production of impressions upon linen by blood, have not yet been concluded ; but we may say here, that we have clearly proved that liquid blood in its normal condition acts strongly upon linen which has been impregnated with aloes, as we shall describe in our final chapter. The spots stand out at first bright-coloured, but almost immediately the edges turn brown, and finally, when the blood is dry, become uniformly dull and dark in tone.

We could, of course, go on to examine in detail other individual blood-marks on the Shroud, perhaps not quite so remarkable as those with which we have already dealt. Thus the spots on the sides of the forehead, among the locks of hair, or on the back of the head, are all positive in appearance. The same may be said of the blood-marks on the left wrist.

With regard to the streams of blood visible on the forearms, we must make a remark the importance of which will be apparent. These blood-streams do not seem to have any connexion with the wounds in the wrists, to which nevertheless they owe their source. It would at first sight seem strange that this should be so, but our inability to understand is no proof of fraud in the impressions. Painters, as a rule, make their representations as clear as possible, and paint things as they see them. To appeal to the general public, an artist's ideas must be simple and easy of comprehension if he wishes his work to be appreciated. The Christ, he would say, had

THE SHROUD OF CHRIST

His hands pierced by nails, and from the wounds made by these nails the blood poured forth. The position of the hands would be higher than the elbows, by reason of the weight of the suspended body, and the blood would therefore flow over the forearms. Some painters have represented this blood like rivers with parallel banks, having their sources in the wounds themselves. Others have represented Christ upon the Cross with His arms extended, horizontally, in which case the blood is shown dropping from the hollows of the hands. In no case, however, do we know of an artist who has intentionally represented blood flowing in streams but having no apparent connexion with the wounds which caused its flow.

Now let this be well noted : every time that we find in the Holy Shroud some strangeness, some departure from tradition, we may feel assured that such strangeness, such departure, can never have been knowingly done by a forger, whose direct intention would have been to appeal forcibly to the imagination of his public. Sometimes, as we shall see, such an apparent error is found in reality to be an absolute truth.

Having said this much, we will return to the observations which we have to make as to the marks of blood on the forearms.

On the upper part of the left wrist some pale thread-like marks are perceptible which join the wound to the stronger brown streams.

The right wrist, as we see, is lying crossed under the left wrist ; the cloth does not touch the wrist, nor indeed the forearm, for some little distance from the wound, from which the blood is flowing. The interruption, then, to which we have alluded is quite natural.

Under the feet we perceive certain brown markings of which the importance is considerable. These are the marks which lead us to conclude that the body, which was wrapped in the Holy Shroud, had the feet pierced with nails in the same manner as the hands. Some of these spots have the edges clearly defined, and not jagged. We conclude therefore that they are produced by dried blood—but they are not all the same. Thus, beside the right foot, that is to say the left in the impression, we see, vaguely, a trifoliate stain or mark, shaped something like a crescent ; careful examination of M. Pia's photographs, reveals that the edges of this spot have a jagged appearance, such as is produced upon a cloth when it is wetted with an albuminous liquid. The mark is not brown enough in colour to represent blood ; it would seem to have more probably been produced by some kind of serum, but it does correspond exactly with the level of the foot.

Under the right heel a dark brown spot corresponds, in part at any rate, with the stains which would be left by a liquid having wetted the cloth; indeed towards the upper part we can see as it were brown filaments which run out horizontally in the stuff.

To us, then, these details are of great interest. If the body which the Shroud enfolded was indeed that of Jesus Christ, the large nails with which the feet had been pierced would have been drawn out of the wounds, when the body was taken down from the cross. Although the sufferer must have been dead for about three hours, a small quantity of blood would have exuded from the wounds, and it is by these exudations that the cloth was tinged at the part where the feet rested; and besides these exudations there are other spots of a different character under the soles of the feet, showing the characteristics of blood which was already dry. One might almost suppose that the trilobed patch which we have just noticed had also been caused by the blood which slowly exuded from the wounds in the feet, before the feet were definitely placed in the position they were to occupy. But we must not linger too long over these minutiæ ; what is really necessary is to show, as we trust we have done, how little the impressions on the Shroud, corresponding with the wounds in the feet, resemble the work of a painter.

Had a forger at that date desired to simulate the wounds made by the nails, he would, we think, have drawn them carefully, showing them in circular form ; the essential thing in his eyes would have been that the wounds should have been easily recognized in the traditional positions. It is for this reason that all painters, even those who clearly had no intention to deceive, have always accentuated the holy wounds. Here we find nothing of the sort. In the right foot the principal clot of blood is manifestly shown under the heel itself, covering altogether the place where the nail had entered, while in the left foot it is also in the neighbourhood of the heel that the blood clots are found ; and the different spots and marks thus shown in no way indicate the classic stigmata. Here again we are forced to abandon the hypothesis of fraud, and to attribute the appearances on the Shroud to accidental and natural causes, in which the intention or imagination of an artist is nowhere discernible.

One word as to the wound on the right shoulder of the body above the shoulder blade, which we have previously attributed to the pressure of the Cross. Once more we find realism. The man would bear the shaft on His back, sustaining the cross-bar with His hands ; under the pressure of the heavy Cross His garment would get pushed into perpendicular folds at the apex of the shoulder. These folds would cut into the flesh and leave on the corpse the marks we see. If this also should be called the work of a painter-forger, how great must have been his ingenuity !

Thus far in our examination we have traced and dealt with, the wounds made by the crown of thorns, the stab from the lance, and the nail wounds in the hands and feet. There now only remain to be examined the somewhat singular markings perceptible on the back and on the fleshy parts of the thighs and calves, which there seems every reason to believe are the marks of violent blows inflicted by some short heavy instrument. If the body be that of Jesus Christ, these wounds or marks would be those of scourging. Had such marks been the work of a forger, he would assuredly have tried to indicate marks such as are usually produced by such punishment.

Let us first of all analyze the shape of one of these marks ; what is true of one may be said to be true of all.

On the back, underneath the right shoulder-blade, and in a comparatively clear space, two of these marks are to be found side by side. Each has the shape of a small piece of stick about three centimetres long, taking into account the scale of the body, and slightly thickened at the two ends. As regards the colour, we may call it of a middle tint, but towards the ends the markings grow darker. We are reminded by its appearance of a small dumb-bell which in striking the body lengthways had left the marks of the two ball-like ends more strongly impressed at the centre than on the borders. At the worst part the skin has been cut and blood has oozed forth, otherwise the spot is pale in colour ; it is certainly a mark produced by serum with which the linen has been wetted, for wounds by which the skin is abrased, dry with difficulty, and may exude serum for some time.

Although nearly all these singular marks on the Shroud can on examination be explained, as we have attempted to explain them, there are two at least which are not easily accounted for. With the aid of the original photographs, especially the positive on glass (i.e. photographic negative), which represents the Shroud in facsimile, we are able to examine very minutely the marks which are of necessity less sharply defined in our reproductions in photogravure. The originals clearly show that the brown centres of the enlarged extremities are not equally distinct, and that the skin has been cut to different depths. And here the precise form, even of that part of the wound which has drawn blood, varies considerably. Thus, on the right calf of the figure, there are three distinct marks which resemble each other only in their general outline. The topmost one has a regular dumb-bell shape, the upper part of which is darkly stained by blood, while in the lower part the tint remains fainter. Below this mark comes another which is irregular in shape and difficult to define. The one lower still is bent as if the metallic instrument by which it was made had been hook-shaped. These details are all perfectly visible on Plate IV. on the left calf of the figure shown in our reproduction.

On the back there are some markings which are not very clearly given in our photogravure. They look like the half of a dumb-bell, as if one end only had made its mark.

All these peculiarities are intensely realistic ; on the one hand it was natural that the metal buttons with which the wounds were inflicted should not be all exactly alike ; on the other hand, one and the same button could not have struck the body exactly in the same way each time.

In our figure 2 will be found at A a drawing which gives the general appearance of the wounds ; next to it, at B, is a reproduction of the probable shape of the piece of metal with which such blows could have been inflicted. About eighteen such wounds may be distinguished on the sacrum, or fleshy parts in the vicinity of the pelvis. These white marks show plainly on Plate V. On Plate IV., which was executed from a different photographic print, they are not so visible. But on the proofs on glass, sent me by M. Pia, the dumb-bell shaped markings are quite apparent, just as we have described them, when looked at transparently.

If, however, the shape of these marks be considered curious, their general distribution and direction in relation to the body are not less interesting. The wounds on the back may be divided into two series. Some, and these are the more numerous, are obliquely marked from top to bottom and from left to right (see Plate v.). They correspond to the direction in which the weapon of the scourger would have descended upon the body were he standing on the left and in the rear of the sufferer. The other series, visible especially on the left shoulder and left side of the back, point in an opposite direction, as if the wielder of the scourge had been standing behind, and on the right of his victim.

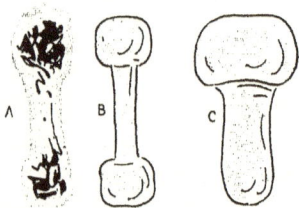

A. TYPE OF WOUND CAUSED BY SCOURGING.
B. SHAPE OF INSTRUMENT CAPABLE OF CAUSING SUCH WOUND.
C. METAL BUTTON ATTACHED TO THE ROMAN "FLAGRUM."
Fig. 2.

The general disposition of the wounds visible on the fleshy parts is also remarkable. They group themselves in a sort of sheaf having a horizontal axis, on each side of which the marks spread outwards.

Blows leaving such marks as these would have been inflicted by a short stick, furnished with a number of thongs, to the ends of which were attached metal buttons. With such a weapon the thongs themselves would not cut the skin, as they would have done without the metal buttons; for these metal buttons would strike the flesh before the thongs could reach it, and immediately after the stroke the scourger would draw back his arm, and lift the thongs in so doing. It may also be noticed that the marks on the back are in an upward direction, while those on the calves are the reverse, as if the scourge had struck the back obliquely from below, upwards; the fleshy parts are marked horizontally, and the calves obliquely, but the strokes in this case are from above, downwards. These marks can all be reproduced by the arm circling from the shoulder, as is done in sprinkling water with a brush.

It is hardly worth while to emphasize how very unlikely it is that any artist having to reproduce the marks of scourging on a human body could have imagined a system of scars so complicated as that which we have here indicated ; each kind of mark would have required special attention, special invention, and we all know how difficult it is to repeat over and over again a representation which, while preserving the same general form, should show infinite variety in detail.

It may be interesting to our readers if we here reproduce an example of work from the hand of a skilled artist show-ing the treatment of this subject, if it be only to realize how difficult it is for a painter, even when aiming at realism, to faithfully depict such a scene, if it has not actually come under his eyes.   Here, in figure 3 is a portion of a very cur-ious work of the fifteenth century, which is preserved in the Gallery at Cologne. The picture is anonymous, but is known as the Passion of Lyversberg.

In the centre of the picture we see Christ crowned with thorns, stricken and buffeted by a set of scoundrels, while in the background are some self-righteous Pharisees who preserve a general air of approval, without any intention of active co-operation in such questionable com-pany. The malignant and brutal realism of the scene cannot be surpassed ; indeed, all the details of the picture are curiously minute and faithful. Evidently, if any one could be found capable of portraying such a punishment, it should be the artist who painted this

THE SCOURGING. BY LE MAITRE DE LA PASSION DE LYVERSBERG, COLOGNE MUSEUM (XV. CENTURY).
Fig. 3.

picture. Notice the truthfulness of gesture with which the scourger raises both his arms, in act to strike ; his back is turned to us, his legs wide apart, so as to give the blow with all his strength, his coat is tied round his loins—the hanging sleeves half pulled inside out in his haste to strip himself, his shirt has bulged loose at his waist through his exertions. On the right of Christ is a head, which by its extraordinary concentration of hatred, shows the insight and imagination of the artist.

But all these great qualities are worthless when we consider the inability of the painter, not merely to give us an adequate representation of the Christ Himself, but even to show us the appearance of the wounds which would be produced by scourging.

The ruffian in shirt-sleeves is brandishing a sort of birch rod—indeed, the ground is strewn with its broken twigs. We should expect the body of Christ to be striped with the strokes, but it is not so ; the artist has chosen to cover the body with little stabs such as might have been made by big pins. These stabs are distributed over the whole surface of the sufferer's body, which would indicate that the punishment had been of long duration. Yet they remain separate from one another, and from each small stab trickles a symmetrical tear of blood. Plainly these wounds could never have been inflicted by a rod such as the artist has chosen, and in no case would the blood have trickled down as the painter has so clumsily and so monotonously represented it. Even the most finished artist of that day is at fault when he has to draw upon his imagination.

The marks of the scourging as shown on the Holy Shroud are all the more interesting and realistic by sheer force of contrast.

A weapon which could have produced such marks corresponds closely to the Roman *flagrum,* as described in the *Dictionary of Roman and Greek Antiquities*, by Anthony Rich. Here also we find the description of the flagellum—another sort of scourge—which it may not be amiss to quote. " *flagellum* (μάστιξ) : a whip made of numerous cords, twisted and knotted like the feelers of a polypus, which indeed are designated by the same name." *Ov. Met.* iv. 367 refers to it as " a whip made with long flexible lashes capable of cutting a man to death." The wounds inflicted by it are always described in words which express the action of cutting, thus, *caedere, secare, scindere*, in contradistinction to the *flagrum*, the action of which is described by such words as *pinsere* and *rumpere*, which give the sense of striking heavily and with force.

Evidently the wounds which we are studying could not have been produced by the *flagellum*. Let us see what is said of the *flagrum* ? " An instrument chiefly used for the punishment of slaves. . . . It was composed of many chains, to each of which a metal button was attached, having a short wooden handle like a postillion's whip ; its blows were rather heavy than cutting." This description is said to be that of one discovered at Herculaneum. There was also the *flagrum talis tessellatum*, which was made of thongs to the ends of which were attached the knuckle-bones (*tali*) of sheep ; but of this we need not speak, as the wound-marks would not correspond with those under consideration.

Clearly then if we eliminate the thonged scourge and the knuckle-bone scourge, we may compare the marks on the Shroud to wounds inflicted by the metal buttons of the *flagrum*. The shape of these buttons was variable. The example given by us in figure 2 is reproduced from a drawing in Rich's *Dictionary*, and differs but slightly from the kind of button to which we have attributed the marks shown in our photographs, being enlarged at one extremity only, instead of being in the shape of a dumb-bell.

The *flagrum* reproduced by Rich is made not of thongs, but of chains, three chains only being fastened to the handle of the scourge, which leads us to think that the buttons were specially large and heavy. Those which we have in mind must have been lighter, for we know that in ordering Christ to be scourged Pilate desired to excite the people's compassion rather than to inflict severe punishment. It must be confessed that although the severity of a blow, the mark of which is only three centimetres long, is not in itself very great, yet, when we consider the number of blows inflicted, it is obvious that the pain endured must have been intense.

If then the wound-marks visible on the Shroud in such perfection of detail are the work of fraud, we must own that the forger was indeed gifted with consummate ability. But even if we admit (for the sake of argument) that he *could* have painted such wound-marks we assert that he *would* not have painted them as they appear upon the Shroud.

The hypothesis of fraud considered from this new aspect, becomes more unlikely than ever.

At the back of the head the clots from the crown of thorns are shown in the places traditionally assigned to them, but it is remarkable how few there are in front. Painters generally have depicted many more, but we will not insist on this point.

Let us glance at the wound in the side. It is shown on the left side in the imprint, because, as we have frequently said, it was on the right side of the actual body. As we know, this interversion was well understood by Giulio Clovio. The forger must have thought of it, too, but he also had to consider his public. It may have been out of deference to popular prejudice that he shows the wound on the right of the Shroud as he would have done in the case of an ordinary portrait, for we must admit that the public of the year 1353 cannot have been very exacting as to scientific accuracy.

Now we come to a more important point. The nail-wound of the left hand is in the wrist, *not* in the centre of the palm, as demanded by tradition. In a forged relic such a parade of independence would scarcely have been tolerated. As it was, to have shown the public only one hand, and consequently only one wound, was remarkable enough. Such licences would be pardoned only in the most authentic relic. Yet anatomy proves that the nails *must* have been driven into the wrists, *not* into the hands. Here again tradition is contradicted.

What would have become of the body on the cross, had the nails been driven through the palms of the hands ? The weight of the body would quickly have enlarged the wounds, and the ligaments at the base of the fingers would soon have given way. If, however, the nails were driven in at the wrist there would be no chance of the wound's enlargement ; indeed, the very weight of the body would throw pressure on the extremities of the metacarpal bones, which are very firmly united. It is easy to verify this experimentally. Let us take the right hand between the four fingers of the left and the thumb, pressing the thumb firmly on the back of the right hand. If we thrust our thumb-nail between the bases of the third and fourth fingers, there is no appreciable resistance. Hence the suppleness of the human hand ; the metacarpal bones turn easily, the one upon the other, when laterally compressed. Let us repeat the experiment, thrusting the thumb-nail this time into the wrist. We could not separate the ligaments of the metacarpal bones here if we tried.

Therefore on the Shroud, had the wound been visible in the centre of the hand, we should think that some painter had been at work, who was more mindful of tradition than of anatomy. As for the wounds in the feet, we have already dealt fully with the appearance of the blood-marks at and near the heels. If the nails were really driven in here, it must have been at the instep ; the wounds in the feet would then exactly correspond to those in the hands. All pictures give the feet pierced in the centre of the metatarsus, just as the hands are given pierced in the centre of the metacarpus, but certainly the feet would have been more solidly fastened had the nail been driven in at the instep.

We cannot, however, exactly determine the position of these wounds, as the front portion of the feet is not shown in the photographs. We shall draw attention, however, in Chapter IV to two copies, dating from the sixteenth century, in which the wounds are represented as near the ankles. The copyists in thus giving them have bravely disregarded tradition, which leads us to believe that the copies must have been made from this actual Shroud itself.

As to the scourge-wounds, there need be no surprise at the strangeness of their shape. The only point on which we lay stress is the improbability of any painter of religious subjects in the Middle Ages venturing to put marks of flagellation on the fleshy part of the body by the pelvis. It is indeed altogether unusual to find a nude Christ, deprived even of the small loin-cloth which is always allowed by artists. In the early centuries Christ was represented on the Cross clothed completely in a robe, but from the twelfth century the robe is shortened, until at last nothing is left on the naked figure but a small loin-cloth. A nude Christ is quite exceptional. The following phrase borrowed from Didron shows us the scandal which arose amongst the believers, and which still exists, at the mere thought of

THE SHROUD OF CHRIST

Christ being represented entirely naked. "In the fourteenth century, and even in our own time, Jesus has been constantly represented on the Cross with only a small piece of linen round the loins ; worse still—terrible thought—Jesus has been represented on the Cross, absolutely naked. Such an absolute nudity of the Divine is a revolting spectacle. I must admit, however, that I know only one such instance of complete nudity. It is in a manuscript in the Royal Library (*Heures du Duc d'Anjou*, fol. 162). I believe that a second instance may be found in the *Biblia Sacra* (No. 6,829), possibly, nay probably, due to an error of the painter." (Didron, *Iconographie Chrétienne, Histoire de Dieu.* Paris, Imprimerie Royale, 1844. 607 pages, 150 figures.)

We can cite another instance of a nude Christ ourselves—a painting by Henri de Bellechose about 1415. The picture is at the Louvre. The custom of depicting Christ in a loin-cloth is so well established that the absence of even this slight clothing has been made use of by critics as a reason for doubting the authenticity of the Holy Shroud. These critics, however, did not perceive that their argument might be turned against themselves. For whom is it inadmissible to represent Christ on the Cross in a nude condition ? For Christians. But the impropriety was even greater in the Middle Ages, for early representations gave the figure completely robed. The Roman soldiers, however, who crucified Christ had no scruples of the sort, nor any respect for Him of any kind.

In Chapter IV we mention other shrouds whereon Christ is represented nude, such as those of Besançon and Xabregas ; but were not these copies of the Holy Shroud of Turin ? The absolute solution of this problem, however, can only be arrived at by an examination of the Shroud itself. There may be a small cloth under the hands, but there is certainly no covering on the back.

A recent author, P. Solaro, has thought that in the photographs there could be found traces of some covering, but he was mistaken. The markings to which he alludes are merely the borders of one of the spots which had been burnt.

Mgr. Colomiatti, in a paper written by him in the *Revue des Sciences Ecclésiastiques*, "Sur l'Authenticité du Saint Suaire de Turin," mentions clearly the absence of any loin-cloth in the original image, and alludes further to the fact that in many of the copies the omission has been rectified. Thus we may conclude that the very nudity of the image on the Holy Shroud goes to prove its authenticity, all the more from the fact that the supposititious forger must be considered to have intentionally laid stress on the circumstance of nudity, inasmuch as he has shown some fifteen scourge-marks on those parts of the body which the loin-cloth would have veiled.

To sum up, the wound-marks visible on the Holy Shroud are not such as the supposititious forger of Lirey would have represented them. Their extreme naturalness and exactness are beyond the conception of human skill. We have the right to deny that the stigmata of Christ are produced fraudulently, just as we have the right to deny that the impressions of the body itself are a fraud.

We approach the conclusion to which all our arguments have been trending. Soon we shall be able to say with certainty, " Yes, the body which the Holy Shroud covered was indeed the body of Jesus Christ."

We must, however, before going further, consider the somewhat singular hypothesis, according to which some man of the Middle Ages, some inhabitant of Byzantium, obtained somewhere and somehow a cloth bearing on it the chemical imprint of a human body, on which he had only to paint the wounds designating Christ in order to produce a most valuable relic. This supposition is only to be equalled by another hardly less singular. The body, it is suggested, by some extraordinary coincidence, perchance already bore the marks of the wounds of Christ, so that there was no need to counterfeit them. Now this presupposes either that the body itself had been marked and prepared fraudulently, or else the body was indeed that of some poor criminal who had died upon the cross, after having been crowned with thorns, scourged, and pierced in the side by a lance.

There is no limit to hypothetical ingenuity. We need only say this. The impressions on the Shroud are such that neither intentionally nor by chance could men. living in the Middle Ages, or before the Middle Ages, have procured such a winding-sheet. We declare that not only could

43

no such cloth have been found in any tomb, but also that not even the happiest combination of circumstances could have led them to discover any method by which such impressions could have been produced from a dead body.

The simple fact remains. No such impression on a winding-sheet has ever been found in any tomb, and we may add that it is materially impossible that such a thing should be found. Whatever may be the exact nature of the chemical process by which the impressions were produced, what concerns us now is the organic action exercised between a naked body and a prepared cloth. All such action is restricted by one essential condition, namely, that the body should have remained in contact with the cloth for too short a time to allow of putrefaction. If corruption set in, any impression previously made would be *ipso facto* destroyed. What indeed is found in a violated sepulchre ? A mummy or a skeleton. In either case the tomb could not have furnished a winding-sheet like the Holy Shroud. On the other hand, it is not possible for any one to have arrived at a method of producing such impressions, and this because of their altogether exceptional character.

It may be asked, Can these impressions be due to some chemical process other than that which is caused by the action of febrile sweat and aloes ? We know of none such. Can they have been produced by the precise chemical change which we shall describe in our final chapter ? Then it would have been necessary to have had assembled by fortuitous chance all the circumstances which we have detailed ; there must have been a body bathed in urenic perspiration and covered with the sweat of feverish agony ; this same body, while still unwashed, must have been covered with a shroud heavily imbued with a mixture of oil and aloes ; and, finally, this same body must have been removed from the tomb without any symptom of putrefaction having been manifest. It is unbelievable.

One by one each argument hostile to authenticity has been met and combated. Have our critics been able to prove that the impressions were painted—wound-marks, modelling and all ? They think not ; and we have now we consider the right to affirm that we are in possession of the actual impression of Christ.

44

THE GOSPELS WITH REGARD TO THE ENTOMBMENT

A STUDY OF THE GOSPELS WITH REGARD TO THE ENTOMBMENT
OF CHRIST

We believe the impressions visible on the Shroud to represent Christ and Him alone. We cannot see that we are deceiving ourselves when we maintain that these are indeed the prints made by His body. And if this is so, since we know the historical conditions of the death of Jesus, we also know that it is legitimate to refer the production of these impressions to the action of febrile sweat on aloes.

And now let us inquire how and why it is that the wonderfully precise conditions which we have defined were all realized at the death of Christ. We will turn to the Gospels for our answer. Commandant Colson has studied them in the original Greek text, and has submitted his readings to an expert.

We shall find that the accounts given in the Gospels agree absolutely with our scientific observations ; and the Gospel narrative will thus complete our work on the Shroud, affording as it were a frame-work to our physico-chemical studies. Our scientific observations in their turn will accentuate the details of a narrative which is somewhat meagre.

The oldest record relative to the burial of Christ is that of St. Matthew. It was written in Hebrew at Jerusalem a few years after the death of Christ, and was translated almost immediately into Greek. We give the English translation from the Revised Version :

" When the even was come there came a rich man of Arimathea, named Joseph, who also himself was Jesus' disciple ; he went to Pilate and begged the body of Jesus. Then Pilate commanded the body to be delivered. And when Joseph had taken the body, he wrapped it in a clean linen cloth, and laid it in his own new tomb, which he had hewn out in the rock ; and he rolled a great stone to the door of the sepulchre and departed " (Matt. xxvii. 57 *et seq.*).

Here is St. Mark's account, written originally in Greek :

" And he bought fine linen and took Him down and wrapped Him in the linen and laid Him in a sepulchre " (St. Mark xv. 46.)

The word *sindon* (a winding-sheet) is twice repeated here ; and the same word appears again in St. Luke's account, written also in Greek :

" And he took it down and wrapped it in linen and laid it in a sepulchre " (Luke xxiii. 53).

These three accounts compiled in different places from the oral tradition handed down from witnesses of the Passion, absolutely agree with each other. We must believe that the corpse was wrapped in a linen cloth of thin material, sufficiently large to envelop the body. There is no question in these narratives of the spices ; it is St. John who, after speaking of the intervention of Joseph of Arimathea, mentions further the part taken by Nicodemus, as follows :

" And there came also Nicodemus (which at the first came to Jesus by night) and brought a mixture of myrrh and aloes, about an hundred pound weight." Joseph of Arimathea and Nicodemus came with the intention of burying Jesus according to the Jewish custom. They brought a mixture of myrrh and aloes which amounted to about thirty-three kilogrammes according to Roman weight. If these two followers of Jesus had immediately proceeded to the complete and final burying of the body they would have carefully washed and anointed it. They would have bound the arms and legs with bandages, intended to keep the spices in place ; they would have wrapped round the head a handkerchief (*sudarium*), which was used to dry the sweat ; finally they would have enveloped the body in the winding-sheet of which the three first gospels make mention. These operations were lengthy, and could not be done all at once. We know by the quotation from St. Matthew that it was already late when Joseph of Arimathea came to Calvary. It would have required time for him to complete the necessary formalities with Pilate, and then to draw the nails and take down the body from the Cross.

Certainly by the time that Christ had been taken down from the Cross the day must have been nearly done ; moreover, it was Friday, the eve of the Sabbath during which day all work was forbidden.

The Sabbath began at six, or half-past six, in the month of April. Therefore it is certain that Joseph of Arimathea and Nicodemus would not have had time to perform a regular burial. They would have been obliged to do what they could in the limited time at their disposal, and postpone till the day after the Sabbath (our Easter Day) the completion of the unfinished obsequies.

This is confirmed by St. Mark, inspired by St. Peter, who, as well as St. John, was an eye-witness of the Passion. Speaking of the holy women, he expresses himself thus :

" And when the Sabbath was past, Mary Magdalene, Mary the mother of James, and Salome had brought sweet spices that they might come and anoint him " (Mark xvi. 1).

The verb ἀλείφω has here a very precise meaning, like the word *ungere* in the Latin text, " Ut venientes ungerent Jesum " ; it signifies to anoint, to smear with, to rub with oil.

St. Luke relates also that the women who came from Galilee with Jesus, after having seen how the body was laid in the sepulchre, bought spices and ointments and came back the day after the Sabbath, bringing the spices with them (see Matt. xxvii. 61 and Mark xv. 47).

If, then, these holy women who had been present at the burial returned on Easter Day to anoint the body, it was because this anointing had not yet been done. In this case the body would also not have been enswathed, as this operation could only be performed after the anointing.

What, then, did Joseph and Nicodemus do with the mixture of myrrh and aloes ? The passages cited hitherto give us no information on this subject. If we had only the accounts given by Matthew, Mark, and Luke we should be free to admit that the linen cloth was without trace of aromatics, but St. John is much more explicit ; this is his account :

" Then took they the body of Jesus,

καὶ	ἔδησαν	αὐτὸ	ὀθονίοις	μετὰ	τῶν	ἀρωμάτων,
and	bound	it	in linen cloths	with	the	aromatics

καθὼς	ἔθος	ἐστὶν	τοῖς	Ἰουδαίοις	ἐνταφιάζειν
as	a custom	is	among the	Jews	to prepare for burial."

The Vulgate gives it thus : " Acceperunt ergo corpus Jesu et ligaverunt illud linteis cum aromatibus, sicut mos est Judaeis sepelire."

What is the exact signification of this verse ? As we read it in the Greek or Latin text the phrase presents no difficulty, but a very different

47

meaning is often attributed to it, a meaning which we cannot accept, as follows. For the due observance of Jewish custom it was necessary that the body should first be anointed and then bound with bandages. Now the Latin word " ligaverunt " might easily be translated as " bound " and the Greek ὀθονίοις (in place of the Latin word " linteis ") signifies " *bands*." In this case the burial would have been complete and definite on the Friday evening, which is contrary to what we learn from the impressions on the Shroud, and also from the other three Gospels.

But let us more closely study the text of St. John.

The Greek word ἔδησαν signifies primarily " to envelop," and this is also the meaning of the Latin expression " ligaverunt " ; why should we then use the word " bound " ?

If we took ὀθονίοις in its strict sense, we should translate it as " little bands or strips " ; but then we should be ignoring the Shroud, which nevertheless was indispensable for the interment. Also we should be disregarding the fact that a little further on St. John establishes himself a precise distinction between *two sorts of linen.*

καὶ θεωρεῖ τὰ ὀθόνια κείμενα καὶ τὸ σουδάριον ὃ ἦν ἐπὶ τῆς κεφαλῆς αὐτοῦ,
and sees the linen-cloths lying and the {handkerchief / napkin} which was upon head his

He seems here to give to the word ὀθόνια a wider sense than " little bands or strips." His meaning would not have been complete if he had used the word " *sindon* " only, because he goes on to tell us that there were *also* linen *clothes*. We are glad of the mention of these linen clothes or cloths, for it will be remembered that the marks on the Shroud indicated that small rolls of linen had been placed between the Shroud and the body, notably on either side of the face. The word ὀθονίοις suits our meaning very well, if taken in its wider sense.

So to take it would accord entirely with the Vulgate, where we find ὀθονίοις fearlessly translated by the word " linteis," a word having a wide meaning. The exact Greek equivalent of *linteis* would be ὀθόναις from ὀθόνη, which means " linen in general." We do not know whether the variant ὀθόναις is found in any of the Greek manuscripts from which the Vulgate was translated. However that may be, a few verses later this same Vulgate goes on to translate ὀθόνιον by " linteamen," signifying in this case " a small band."

The preposition μετά, followed by the genitive, expresses the idea of accompaniment and participation ; it is used in this way by St. John (see John xx. 7). It in no wise indicates that the spices and aromatics were used to anoint the body. If, then, we remember that Joseph of Arimathea and Nicodemus were in haste, it would seem natural to admit that as they could do no better, they had at least poured the mixture upon the cloth. Presuming that this is what happened, we get the exact meaning of the word μετά ; the aromatics would be " in conjunction with " the linen.

In that case we might say that the essentials of Jewish custom had actually been observed, inasmuch as that a shroud had been used, and also a mixture of myrrh and aloes.

Everything considered, the result of our observations is to corroborate the literal meaning of the Vulgate ; the accounts given in the four Gospels harmonize with each other and bear out all that we have said. We are fully able to maintain the ground already gained by our scientific observation of the Shroud.

Let us now turn to what happened on the morning of Easter Day.

The holy women, having come early to the sepulchre to anoint the body, and finding the tomb empty, went at once to tell St. Peter and St. John ; St. John is the first to reach the sepulchre, but he does not enter it.

We should like here to refer our readers to our article in the *Revue Chrétienne* of July 1. We find that in this article we unconsciously replied to a work by M. Bouvier published in *La Quinzaine* of the same date. M. Bouvier's readers will perceive that he actually strengthens our arguments in trying to refute them, inasmuch as he translates St. Mark's ἀλείψωσιν quite incorrectly, thus making three of the Gospels to directly contradict the fourth, as does also M. Piraux.

Let us re-read the seventh verse. The narrator, an eye-witness, marks the distinction between the cloths left in the tomb.

THE SHROUD OF CHRIST

First, the ὀθόνια, with which we are already acquainted; the word ὀθόνιον signifies in general " small pieces of linen," more particularly " small bandages "—bands, strips.

Second, the σουδάριον, or Shroud; and that is all.

The first lay on the ground in disorder; there is no difficulty about them. As for the word σουδάριον, it has generally been considered to indicate the small handkerchief placed on the head of the corpse, but we, as we have said, are unable to accept this interpretation.

Indeed, if " the napkin " of St. John *were* the face-kerchief, where would have been the Shroud (*sindon*)? St. John would not have made mention of it.

Moreover the expressions used by the writer prove to us that this σουδάριον was neither more nor less than the Shroud (*sindon*) itself.

Verse 5. καὶ   παρακύψας   βλέπει   κείμενα   τὰ   ὀθόνια,   οὐ   μέντοι   εἰσῆλθεν
  and stooping down he sees   lying   the linen-cloths not however he entered

Verse 6. ἔρχεται   οὖν   Σίμων   Πέτρος, . . . καὶ   θεωρεῖ   τὰ   ὀθόνια   κείμενα
  comes   then   Simon   Peter   and   sees   the linen-cloths   lying

Verse 7. καὶ   τὸ   σουδάριον   ὃ   ἦν   ἐπὶ   τῆς   κεφαλῆς   αὐτοῦ,   οὐ   μετὰ
  and   the { handerchief } which was upon   head   his   not   with
          { napkin }

τῶν ὀθονίων κείμενον, ἀλλὰ χωρὶς ἐντετυλιγμένον εἰς ἕνα τόπον (St. John xx. 5, 6, 7.)
the linen-cloths lying   but by itself folded up   in a place

Read the Greek phrase, " The Shroud was ἐντετυλιγμένον εἰς ἕνα τόπον." the preposition εἰς with the accusative, indicating movement; this expression signifies that the linen " had been rolled up in a bundle, and put in one place." It is not, then, a mere handkerchief or face cloth; it must have been a long band of cloth which could be rolled up like a carpet, beginning at one end and finishing at the other; when this had been done the whole linen would be " wrapped together in a place by itself."

It may be argued that only the usual " suaire " or sweat-cloth is alluded to, because St. John specifies that the σουδάριον had been placed on " the head of Jesus." No doubt it *was* " on the head," but it was also " over the head." The preposition ἐπὶ with the genitive signifies " over " as well as " on." The long winding-sheet passed actually over the head of Christ

50

(see Plate I.), and by the fact of thus passing served as a kerchief or face-cloth.

The Latin version is less forcible, but agrees word for word with the Greek : " 5. Et cum se inclinasset, vidit posita linteamina, non tamen introivit. 6. Venit ergo Simon Petrus sequens eum, et introivit in monumentum, et vidit linteamina posita. 7. Et sudarium, quod fuerat super caput ejus, non cum linteaminibus positum, sed separatim involutum in unum locum. 8. Tunc ergo introivit et ille discipulus, qui venerat primus ad monumentum ; et vidit et credidit."

Here we find a distinction made between the " linteamina," which correspond to the Greek ὀθόνια (and which signify also bandages), and the sudarium. The first were placed on the ground, " posita," while the napkin was rolled up in a place by itself, " involutum in unum locum." The preposition " in," followed by the accusative, shows the movement of the person during the act of rolling. The preposition " super " signifies " over," like the Greek ἐπί.

It is clear from the literal examination that we have here made of the Greek and Latin texts, that the accounts given by the four Evangelists fully agree with and support each other. We must not forget that amongst the Jews all linen used in burial was held to be impure, and the fact of its preservation would therefore be a most carefully guarded secret amongst the disciples.

A closer agreement between the results of a physico-chemical study, made after a lapse of twenty centuries, and the testimony of those who were actual witnesses of the events, could not be desired. Let us summarize in a few sentences such circumstances of Christ's enshroudment as are brought out by our inquiry.

At the moment of death the body of Christ was covered with wounds and feverish sweat. After the disciples had taken down the body from the Cross they caried it to the sepulchre and enveloped it in a great shroud, as we see in Plate I. This shroud was impregnated with a mixture of oil and aloes, but the body had neither been washed nor anointed. In the sepulchre small rolls of linen supported the head at each side. The impressions on the Shroud were produced by the ammoniacal emanations from the body as we shall describe in Chapter VII. From some of the wounds exudations of serum soiled the linen, while the clots of blood produced, in places, specially marked imprints.

On the morning of Easter Day, according to the Gospels, the sepulchre was found empty, the small rolls of cloth being on the ground and the large Shroud rolled up by itself. These facts are testified to by the holy women, and by the disciples, Peter and John.

We shall show scientifically that the body did not remain enveloped in the Shroud more than two or three days.

We will now see what History has to say about the Holy Shroud.

TRANSLATOR'S NOTE.—Skeat gives the derivation of napkin as " nappe," cloth or table-cloth, which again is " linen in its larger sense."

CHAPTER III

DOCUMENTARY HISTORY OF THE HOLY SHROUD

WE confess that documentary history is distinctly *un*favourable to the authenticity of the Holy Shroud, and it is on this lack of historical testimony that the opposition, dating from the fourteenth century onwards, has been based. The relic had lost its passports on its long journey, and what we have to do now is to search for them. If no proofs are to be found, if we cannot discover what became of the Shroud before 1200, and above all between 1205 and 1353, we shall be obliged to relinquish all hope of supporting our case by historical evidence ; and the claim of the Holy Shroud will rest entirely on scientific probability.

We will, therefore, try to give our readers a categorical chronology of the Holy Shroud, and we will borrow our material for the most part from its chief opponent, M. le Chanoine Chevalier !

The recorded history of the Shroud of Turin (Lirey) commences in the year 1353, when Geoffroy the First, count of Charny, and lord of Champagne, presented the relic to the abbey of Lirey, which had been founded by him in the vicinity of the town of Troyes. This nobleman was Governor of Picardy, and had accompanied the Dauphin, Humbert II, in the crusade of 1346. There is absolutely nothing to prove that the relic was brought back by him from the East. In 1355 Count Geoffroy was appointed Grand Standard Bearer by King John II of France, and was slain beside his King, on September 19, 1356, at the battle of Poitiers.

As Geoffroy, count of Charny, gives no precise account of how the sacred relic came into his possession, we fear that its history can never be absolutely traced back earlier than 1353. The Charny family merely said that the Holy Shroud had been obtained as spoils of war or had been received by the Count as a reward of valour ; and it must even be admitted that so far no actual record or deed recording the donation of the relic to the monks of Lirey has been discovered.[1]

M. de Mély in *La Revue Critique* of December 24–31, 1900, cites " a letter of indulgence signed by twelve bishops, who in 1357 granted privileges to those who should come on certain specified days to offer their veneration to the relics of the abbey," relics of which a list is given, and among which the Shroud is not mentioned, although the year 1357 was the year after Count Geoffroy's death. But M. de Mély has however omitted to mention that in 1355 the Charny family reassumed the charge of the sacred relic, and that it remained in their keeping until 1389. Again, mention is made of the record kept at the Abbey of masses said for the soul of the defunct Count Geoffroy, in which no mention is made of the relic ; but it should have been added that the record makes no special mention of specific gifts, but merely recalls the memory of the Count as a " benefactor of the Abbey." That the Shroud was not mentioned by the Comte de Charny proves nothing. Let us *suppose* that he did not *wish to say* how it came into his family's possession. He would certainly have maintained a prudent silence with regard to it.

It may be as well to inquire here whether at the date 1353 there was known, if not the Holy Cloth of Lirey, any shroud or burial-cloth said to have been used as the Shroud of Christ. We have but to refer to page 9 of the *Revue Critique*, cited above, to find a series of extracts, of which the most ancient takes us back to the year A.D. 670. In some of these there is mention of a face-cloth (*sudarium*) as having been folded round the head of the dead Christ ; in others the word " sindon " (winding-sheet) is used, or the Shroud is spoken of simply as cloth (*linges*).

It was in the eleventh century that pilgrims began to make mention of the burial-clothing of our Lord Jesus Christ as being among the relics in the possession of the Emperor at Byzantium. In 1150 an English pilgrim specifies one of these relics as " Sudarium quod fuit super caput ejus," while in 1171 William of Tyre expressly mentions " syndonem." Thus in twenty-one years a small kerchief (*sudarium*) has become " syndonem,"

[1] Historians may well refuse to accept as historically probable the authenticity of a relic which has so little testimony to prove its origin.

a winding-sheet, which shows that too much importance must not be attached to the words of these ancient writers. The most interesting notice, perhaps, as it is the latest, is that of the Chronicler, Robert de Clary in 1203. I quote from Monsieur Chevalier : " . . . Et entre ches autres en eut j (un) autre des moustiers, que on apeloit Medame Sainte Marie de Blakerne, où li Sydoines, là où Nostre Sires fut envolepés, i estoit, qui cascuns devenres se drechoit tous drois, si que on i pooil bien veïr le figure Notre Seigneur ; on ne seut on onques, ne grieu, ne Franchois, que chis Sydoines devint, quand le vile fu prise " (" And among others there was a monastery called our Lady Sainte Marie de Blakerne, where were the Cloths in which our Lord was wrapped, on which when one stood straight up could plainly be seen the figure of our Saviour. Since then no one, either Greek or French, can say what became of the cloth after the town was taken "). This record is of the highest importance. There was then, we see, at Constantinople, in 1200, in the Imperial Chapel, a shroud (not a face-cloth) which was at that time venerated as the actual Shroud of Christ, and on this winding-sheet when one stood straight up was visible the impression of the figure of the Saviour. And now, if we allow ourselves to suppose that the relic of Constantinople is identical with that of Turin, and it is stretched against a wall, it would be necessary to " stand straight up " in order to see the head clearly, as doubtless the feet would be raised above the ground level. Note further that in the report of Robert de Clary it is clearly stated that at the sack and taking of Constantinople in 1205 by the Latins the winding-sheet was lost, and no one knew what had become of it.

For those of our readers to whom our coming studies and arguments may bring conviction I mention an hypothesis put forward by the Rev. Father Solaro (see chap. vi. pp. 24-27 in his *La S. Sindone*, etc.) to account for the hiatus in the history of the Holy Shroud between the years 1205 and 1353. It is but a supposition, which cannot be proved, but which we will take for what it is worth, admitting that there is no reliable evidence to show that the Shroud of Constantinople *is* identical with that of Lirey. For us, however, who are endeavouring to trace back the Lirey Shroud to the time of our Saviour's crucifixion, P. Solaro's hypothesis is important, especially as the description of the Shroud at Constantinople, slight as it is, would apply equally well to the Shroud of Lirey.

The reasoning of Father Solaro is as follows. The Crusaders sacked the city of Constantinople, but respected the shrine of St. Marie de Bla-kerne ; this is an historic fact, and is testified to by Count Riant in his *Exuviae.* Garnier de Trainel, bishop of Troyes, who accompanied the expedition, was charged with the duty of preserving all the relics which had been found in the Imperial Chapel. Count Riant assures us that the Bishop had full power over these relics, and dealt with them as seemed best to him. A considerable number of valuables and relics were sent by the Bishop to Europe, and the list thereof is known, but in the list there is no mention of the Holy Shroud. Father Solaro supposes that the precious relic was preserved by the Bishop for himself, perhaps for greater security during the homeward journey ; but unfortunately it happened that the Bishop never returned—he died at Constantinople in the year 1205. What, then, became of the Holy Shroud ? Did it pass into the possession of one of the Bishop's subordinates ? the names of most of these are known ; they were chiefly natives of Champagne ; one of them at least was related to the Count de Charny. Thus then the Shroud might have passed surrepti-tiously into the possession of the Count's family ; but we must once more admit that this is probability, and not proof.

Monsieur Chevalier in his pamphlet of 1902 is somewhat contemptuous in his treatment of Father Solaro's hypothesis. He says : " How is it possible, if the Bishop of Troyes had in his keeping, and at his disposal, a relic of the highest sanctity, such as the Holy Shroud, that he did not endow his own cathredral therewith, instead of allowing it to pass into the possession of an unimportant nobleman like the Count de Charny ? How could so holy a relic be transmitted to the West from Constantinople with-out an attestation in due form of its authenticity ? Above all, how could so sacred a relic, when it finally reached France, remain for one hun-dred and fifty years without becoming an object ' of veneration and worship ? "

These questions are reasonable, but it will be noted that Monsieur Chevalier does not allude to the fact of the Bishop's death and the conse-

quent probability of so valuable an object having passed surreptitiously
into the possession of one of his followers.

Let us now proceed with the authentic history of the Holy Shroud
subsequent to 1353. We find the then Bishop of Troyes, Henri de Poitiers,
opposing himself to and discouraging pilgrimages to the shrine on account
of the doubtful authenticity of the relic. " It was taken out of the treasury
of the Abbey, and was no doubt returned to the family of its donor, in
whose keeping it remained during the subsequent troubled years, when
Champagne was ravaged by war and pestilence. In fact, for the next
thirty-four years nothing more was heard of it " (*Étude Critique*, p. 24).

During this time it must be borne in mind that the Shroud remained
in the keeping of the Charny family at St. Hippolyte on the banks of the
river Doubs. In the year 1389 the solemn public display of the relic was
resumed, and again forbidden by episcopal authority. Soon after we find
a new Bishop of Troyes, Pierre d'Arcis, the third in succession from Henry
of Poitiers, and either he or the authorities of the Abbey were menaced
by threats of excommunication on account of the relic. A legal *procès*
was commenced by order of Pope Clement VII of Avignon, in which the
Abbot of Lirey and the Charny family, represented by Count Geoffroy II,
were on one side, and the Bishop of Troyes on the other. The rights of the
Abbey of Lirey were energetically defended, but, as Monsieur Chevalier
gives it (p. 26), " the Bishop did not consider himself beaten, and although
worsted in the lawsuit he assembled a commission of learned theologians,
and published a detailed examination of the whole question. It was held
therein that the Shroud of Lirey was not the true winding-sheet of Christ,
but only a painted representation, the work of man ; and, further, that any
public exhibition of the Shroud was likely to expose the feeble and ignorant
to the perils of idolatry. This memorandum was forwarded to Clement VII
about the close of the year 1389."

According to Monsieur Chevalier, this ecclesiastical pronouncement
settles finally the question of the authenticity of the Shroud of Lirey. It
is indeed a most formidable attack. The Bishop of 1389 recalls the fact
that in 1353 his predecessor, after careful inquiry, had obtained a confession
of the fraud from the forger himself, and proceeds : " Et tandem solerti

diligencia precedente et informacione super hoc facta, finaliter reperit fraudem et quomodo pannus ille artificialiter depictus fuerat, et probatum fuit eciam per artificem qui illum depinxerat, ipsum humano ope factum, non miraculose confectum vel concessum " (*Étude Critique*, Doc. G, p. 8). There, says Monsieur Chevalier, is the avowal of the actual forger himself. What more can be desired ?

We are not disposed to admit so easily an " ex parte " statement. The imputations and assumptions of the Bishop's inquiry—nay, the very avowal of the so-called forger—are worthless if we are able to prove that the impressions on the Shroud cannot have been painted, but are of the nature of a photographic negative. Further still, we find as a result of the much vaunted inquiry, that the Bishop got no satisfaction—" de plus le pape imposait à l'évêque *perpetuum silentium* sur cette question " (*Étude Critique*, p. 25).

We may be allowed to point out that the archives of Troyes must have been very badly kept when there is to be found no written record of any public disavowal of the relic. The Pope's letters on the subject make no mention of any such formal prohibition : he contents himself by re-enforcing his mandate of " perpetual silence " to the Bishop : " Eidem episcopo super inhibitione praedicta perpetuum silentium imponentes " (*Étude Critique*, p. 21).

Indeed, had the authorities of the Abbey of Lirey, together with the Charny family, been guilty of the attempt to foist upon the religious world a manufactured relic they would have been well deserving of censure, if not of excommunication, but the Holy Father Clement VII decides mildly that the relic shall be regarded with veneration as " a copy " of the original. This was perhaps a wise decision, in view of the fact that the previous history of the relic could not be traced.

But the so-called " avowal of forgery by the forger himself " is no longer regarded seriously. It is not surprising that Pierre d'Arcis had no official document to send to Pope Clement VII, and therefore had to publish and send his own examination, because there never had been a legal *procès* in 1355. Pierre d'Arcis himself, in his letter to the Pope, admits this (*Étude Critique*, de M. Chevalier, Appendix, Doc. G, p. 8, lines 15–20).

When the Bishop offers to prove his words, whose testimony does he invoke ? " Le bruit public " ! Is Henry de Poitiers any more reliable as a witness ? M. Chevalier himself seems to say that he is not, for hardly a year later than the date when Henry of Poitiers is supposed to have surprised the authorities of the Abbey in their trickery, " il confirmait avec éloges leur pieux établissement " ! ! (*Ibidem*, p. 23, lines 3-4).

In 1418 the ecclesiastical authorities of Lirey (who now since the mandate of Clement VII recognized their relic as *a copy* of the Holy Shroud) confided the Shroud to the care of the son-in-law and successor of Count Geoffroy II of Charny—Humbert, count of La Roche, and lord of Villersexel and Lirey (*Étude Critique*, p. 31 and following pages). Count Humbert's widow, Marguerite de Charny, obstinately refused to restore the relic, and finally, to avoid further anxiety on the subject, she made it over to the Duke of Savoy. Little by little the doubts and disputes as to the authenticity of the relic, which had so agitated the religious world in 1355-1389, subsided, or were forgotten, and the relic grew in renown. On June 11, 1502, the Holy Shroud was solemnly deposited in the Chapel of Chambéry Castle, where it remained until 1532, when the Chapel was partly destroyed by a fire, in which the Holy Shroud was nearly lost, and of which it bears traces at the present time. In 1534 it was religiously repaired, and finally, in 1578, it was conveyed to Turin, where it has remained ever since.

So then, the linen winding-sheet of Turin, formerly the Holy Shroud of Lirey, presents itself to us as truly remarkable, from a scientific point of view, but without any historical guarantee of authenticity. The history of that piece of linen must be deciphered from its own folds and markings, and the reader will judge whether that history is not marked out with startling clearness, as we hold it to be. How, then, shall we sum up the researches which have been undertaken, and which we have endeavoured to set forth here in detail. We cannot regard the results as hypothetical, for the coincidences are so numerous as to be intensely striking. It is no hypothesis to say that the impressions on the Shroud are of the nature of a photographic negative. We shall demonstrate that beyond any question of doubt. We shall show also that the impressions on the Shroud are not paintings, nor can they be attributed in any way directly to the hand of man. Again, it is no mere hypothesis that the impressions bear unmistakably the wounds of Christ ; but it is, we submit, absolutely hypothetical to say that while the imprint of the body may have been produced by chemical means, the marks of the wounds have been afterwards made by man's hand. In short, our essay is not a sheaf of suppositions, but the logical outcome of scientific investigation, and we venture to predict that the Holy Shroud will obtain definite historical recognition through the opening of the door to scientific investigation.

CHAPTER IV

DESCRIPTIONS OF VARIOUS COPIES OF THE HOLY SHROUD

" WHAT were the impressions on the Holy Shroud three, four and five hundred years ago ? " is the question which we must try to answer next.

Testimony gleaned from this far-off period is by no means to be despised. We have worked at our own investigations chiefly from photographs which we believe that we can interpret ; but the men of the Middle Ages had this great advantage over us : they could examine the Shroud itself. There were other pretended Shrouds, to which were ascribed all the authenticity which we attribute to the relic of Turin. We must examine their pretensions. Good evidence is often obtained even from a bad witness. As a matter of fact, among the shrouds, so-called holy, known in the past, only one can be considered as a serious rival to the Holy Shroud of Turin, namely, the Holy Shroud of Besançon, which was destroyed, as we have seen, by ecclesiastical authority. The linen cloths, venerated at Cadouin, at Cahors, at Compiègne and other places bore no impression of any kind, and therefore need not be considered. Moreover they have been well and fairly dealt with by Monsieur Chevalier in his *Étude Critique*, already referred to. We will mention the false shroud of Xabregas, near Lisbon, in its proper place. It had a local reputation, founded on an absurd legend.

As to the Holy Faces, i.e. the so-called portraits of our Lord on hand-kerchiefs, napkins, or face-cloths, we can give no information. The two which are preserved at Rome have not been photographed, and the painted copies are of no interest. They are all positive paintings.

We will now set forth what is known of the Holy Shroud of Besançon, thereby proving that it was neither more nor less than an imperfect " replica " of the Holy Shroud of Turin.

THE SHROUD OF CHRIST

I

In 1794 the French Convention ordered the Holy Shroud of Besançon to be destroyed; but although the cloth no longer exists, we shall endeavour to give a full and sufficient idea of its appearance by the aid of certain precise descriptions of it and a few very faithful copies which have been preserved.

This particular Holy Shroud was a piece of cloth eight feet long and four feet wide, as set forth in the *History of the Church of Besançon* by Dunod (vol. i. p. 412). On this cloth was plainly visible a picture or representation of Jesus Christ, which in its main lines corresponded with the front aspect of the impression on the Holy Shroud of Turin.

To arrive at the history of the Holy Shroud of Besançon, the information supplied by Chifflet (page 53) is insufficient. He assures us that the relic reached France between the years 1051 and 1253. He supports this assertion by a quotation from a record from the church of St. Étienne, with which we are ourselves familiar : " Quin et ipse S. Leo IX Pontifex maximus, qui anno MXLVIII Ecclesiam S. Stephani majus altare consecravit, in Diplomate, quod deinde Anno MLI canonicis concessit, ait, vidisse se in altari basilicae S. Stephani condidisse pretissimum S. Stephani brachium, ictibus lapidandium Judaeorum quassatum ; nulla prorsus sacrosancti lintei facta mentione ; quod tamen si illic jam fuisset, et ipse oculis lustrasset, non videbatur omissurus. Statim vero post initium saeculi decimitertii, tangitur ritus ostentionis S. Sudarii, ex altari S. Stephani, die Paschae, in quodam Rituum codice, quem scriptum constat ante unionem Ecclesiarum S. Joannis et S. Stephani factum anno MCCLIII."

But this does not mean much. It is not a question here of a portrait of Christ ; besides, there is nothing to prove, in the old record quoted, that the reference is to a Shroud esteemed to be authentic. It is well known indeed that in many churches, at the Easter services, a piece of cloth, like a winding-sheet, was used in ceremonial, simply to bring the scene of the Passion more vividly before the multitude.

Nor can we attach greater importance to the statements of Monsieur

DESCRIPTIONS OF COPIES OF THE HOLY SHROUD

Jules Gauthier, in his *Notes Iconographiques sur le Sainte Suaire de Besançon*. He knows of no allusion to this Shroud before 1523.

There are in the Library of Besançon two dissertations in manuscript, written the one in favour of, the other in opposition to, the authenticity of the relic. We will make use of both. The first (urging its authenticity), was written at the beginning of the eighteenth century, and its writer seems to have had access at the time to documents which it would be necessary to examine anew, if the question had really to be gone into closely. He tells us how the Holy Shroud of Besançon was given to Count Otho de la Roche in 1205, as a recompense for his valour at the siege of Constantinople, the dukedoms of Athens and of Thebes being conferred upon him at the same time. Count Otho sent the precious relic to his father, Pontius de la Roche, who, after showing it to his friends and neighbours, solemnly deposited the sacred object in the hands of Amadeus archbishop of Besançon.

But, in the first place, it is unlikely that a simple French gentleman would have been made a present of so precious a relic as the actual Shroud of our Saviour, bearing His impression; (in Chapter II we set forth all that is known of this Byzantine piece of cloth, giving the testimony of the chronicler Robert de Clary, which directly contradicts the above story. See page 55).

In the second place, we shall see that a singular circumstance happened in the fourteenth century, which would lead us to think that the linen cloth known later as the Holy Shroud of Besançon was altogether different from that known in the thirteenth centry.

Dunod, in his *History of the Church of Besançon*, speaks of the Holy Shroud preserved in the Cathedral of St. Étienne in the thirteenth century, and proceeds thus : " In March, 1349, the church was destroyed by fire, and the box in which the Holy Shroud was kept, seemingly without much formality, was lost. Some years afterwards the relic was found again by a happy chance, " and to make sure that it was the same as was formerly venerated in the church of St. Étienne, it was laid upon a dead man, who immediately revived. The fact of this miracle is established not only by the records of the church of Besançon, but also by a manuscript, preserved up to the present time in the church of St. James, at Rheims, where it had been placed by Richard La Pie, senior priest of Besançon, in the year 1375, who had been himself an eye-witness." (Pages 419–421 of Dunod.)

From so much confused matter we glean certain facts.

In the thirteenth century there was at Besançon a Holy Shroud.

In 1349 this Shroud was burnt.

Some years after, it reappeared, or was replaced by another.

This other, subsequent to 1349, prior to 1375, was simply a copy of the Holy Shroud of Turin, as we shall show.

Figure 4 gives us the Shrouds of Besançon and of Turin drawn side by side, and is taken from an engraving in the work by M. Chifflet, already mentioned. The general attitude of the bodies is the same in both, with one notable exception : in the Besançon Shroud the hands are crossed in an unnatural manner ; in that of Lirey (Turin) the left hand conceals the right ; in that of Besançon both are shown. In the Lirey (Turin) Shroud the body is covered with bleeding wounds ; in that of Besançon the places of the stigmata only are roughly marked out. The inscription on the engraving from Chifflet's work shows us how it was attempted to explain the apparently contradictory appearance of two Christ Shrouds, both bearing the holy image, and how it was that the wounds on the body did not present the same appearances.

This is the inscription : " Lindon Taurinensis refert corpus Christi cruentum et recens de Cruce depositium ; Sudarium vero Bisontinum exhibet illud idem iam lotum ac perunctum et in sepulchro compositum," explaining that the Holy Shroud of *Turin* was the cloth in which the body was wrapped after it was taken down from the Cross, whilst that of *Besançon* was the clothing used in the sepulchre. On the cloth of Lirey (Turin) the traces would be from recent blood and sweat ; those of Besançon would have been produced from the oils and spices used at the entombment. It had been well thought out. But apparently it had not occurred to any one to ask why, at the entombment, there had been no cloth under as well as over the body ? Perhaps they supposed that the other half of the Shroud had been lost !

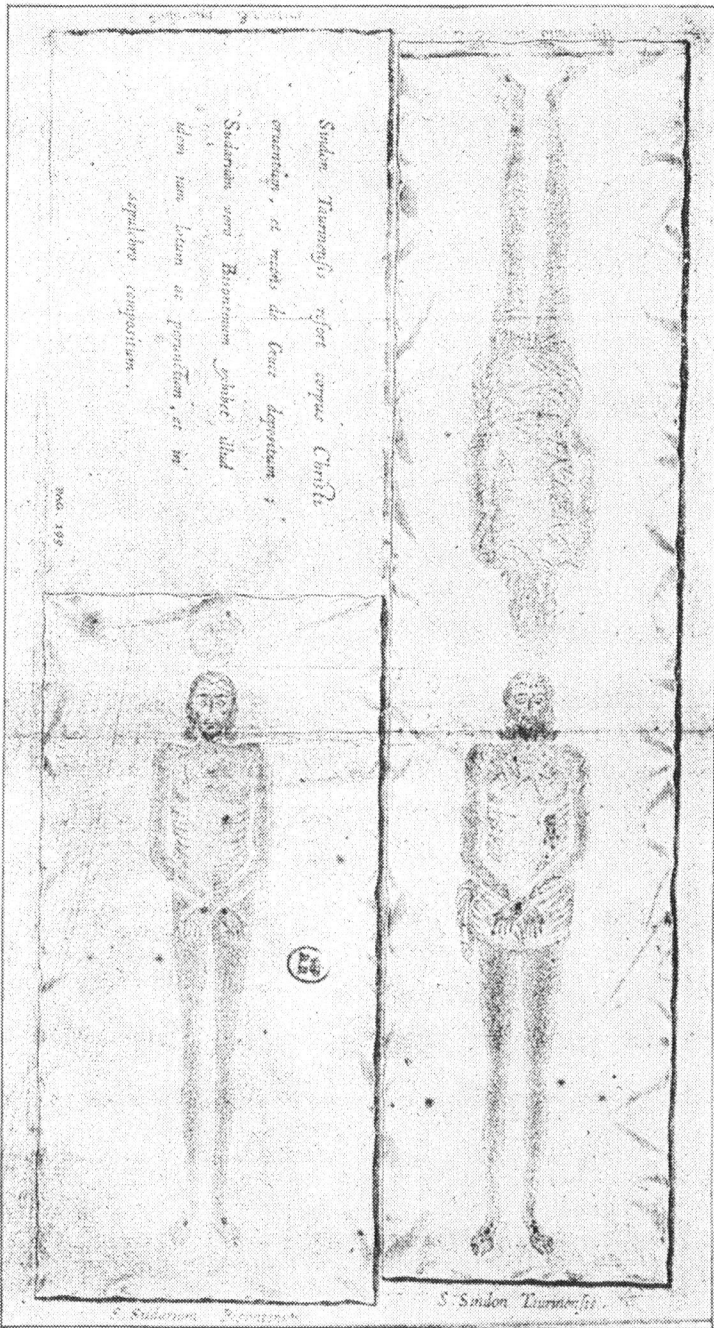

THE BESANÇON AND TURIN SHROUDS, SIDE BY SIDE. FROM AN ENGRAVING IN CHIFFLET'S WORK.
Fig. 4.

65

THE SHROUD OF CHRIST

It is impossible to judge of the artistic or scientific value of the impressions visible on the Holy Shroud of Besançon, from the Chifflet engraving. Clearly it has no artistic merit as given here. But its fellow, the image of Turin, executed by the same draughtsman, has just as little. It is so easy to see that this would-be copy of the Lirey (Turin) Shroud is not at all like the original, that we may well conclude that the same may be said of the Besançon Shroud as sketched here. If it had not been for the awkward misplacing of the hands we might almost have been tempted to believe that the two copies were from one original. In both the drawing is bad, the shoulders high and pointed, the pelvis not shown, the legs out of proportion and stiffly drawn. In both the limbs are modelled in negative, for the shadows grow darker as they approach their centres. The back and breast, on the contrary, are given in positive. On both figures, the nose is shown in negative, and the remaining features in positive. From every point of view the work is mean and insignificant. If then the copy of the Holy Shroud at Besançon, as Chifflet shows it to us, is so bad, what was the original like ? This question must be answered before going further, and to do so we must avail ourselves of the information contained in the other manuscript we spoke of, which was written *against* its authenticity. This is preserved in the Besançon Library as No. 826, and was written some time in the latter half of the eighteenth century.

Its author begins by arguing that the stigmata on the Besançon Shroud are very badly indicated. " But why," he says " are the wounds on the head made by the crown of thorns, only dimly visible ? How is it that not the least mark of scourging can be seen ? The arms and chest could not have escaped being flayed by the lash, and yet the marks left by those portions of the body are *not* stronger than the marks from the legs and thighs. None of these details have been forgotten in the Holy Shroud of Turin. Why did not the blood which flowed down from the wound in the side leave no stain, as it did on the wound itself and its immediate vicinity ?—as it did also in the clots painted like drops on the hands and feet. If the body had been washed, is it likely that the marks of blood would have been washed away in some places and left in others ? " (Folio 60.)

DESCRIPTIONS OF COPIES OF THE HOLY SHROUD

He then expresses surprise that only the front aspect of the body should appear, and points out that in the Shroud of Turin there are both front and back impressions (folio 61). He considers the image of Besançon to be as unnatural in form as it is ugly in appearance, and adds : " Why are these impressions drawn with such regularity ? The human body is not made like a stick, straight up and down ; the shoulders should be broader than the head, the neck, less wide than the loins or the knees. The head of a man is spherical, not flat like a mirror ; the features, the nose in particular, stand out in relief, some higher, some lower than others. The cloth which covered the sacred countenance of Jesus Christ could not have been in contact with all its parts alike. Yet all the impressions are of equal strength. The feet appear to be separated. Yet, surely, they were laid together. The whole figure is in Gothic taste, as I shall proceed to show " (folios 61 and 62).

In folio 65 the author goes on : " In the Holy Shroud the shoulders are shown perfectly square, whilst all the extremities are practically straight lines, just as they are in ancient paintings and stained glass windows in churches of Gothic architecture, good taste, and truth to nature being alike ignored. All which goes to prove that the impression on the Holy Shroud is not natural." [1]

We may quote the passage where our unknown author tells us that in the actual Shroud of Besançon the wound in the breast was shown on the right side, not on the left as Chifflet has it. " On the surface of the Holy Shroud, which has the wound on the right side, it is more distinctly marked than on the other surface. The same with the wounds on the feet and hands. Yet it was not this surface which touched the Holy Body, for then the right side would appear to be the left, just as it is in a print taken from a woodcut or in the reflection in a mirror, showing on the left what is in reality on the right. The artist should have remembered that the impressions on the Holy Shroud would have been stronger on the

---

[1] The two manuscripts " for and against " were written at different dates. The second has this remark, " Je tiens de M. l'abbé Trouillet que cette dissertation est le résultat de conférences entre lui, le premier professeur Bullet et l'abbé Fleury, chanoine de Sainte Magdeleine."—Signé : Grappin.

surface which touched the Holy Body. He has preferred to conform to the pictures of Christ which represent the wound as being on the right side " (folio 64).

Evidently in Chifflet's print it was necessary to put the wound on the left, as they wished to make the figure of Besançon confirm that of Turin, where the wound certainly is on the left side.

We lay stress upon all these blunders, for it is by such that a forger betrays himself. If the clerical contemporaries of Voltaire, who examined the so-called Holy Shroud of Besançon with such open minds, could return to life, we should beg them to criticize freely the Shroud of Turin, feeling sure that their conclusions would be different from those which they arrived at, with regard to the cloth of Besançon.

Let us now return to our examination. It was not only by clumsiness that the author of the Besançon Shroud failed to imitate his model ; he did more ; he pandered to his public. Thus he not only painted the wound on the breast on the right side of the body, and twisted the hands until both were visible, but he deliberately placed in the middle of each hand the marks of the nails, which in the Holy Shroud of Lirey (Turin) are distinctly visible in the wrists.

It may be argued that in Chifflet's engraving the wound is not exactly in the centre of the hands, neither is it in the wrists ; but Chifflet in his description of the Shroud at Besançon asserts that the nails must have pierced the metacarpal bone.

The anonymous author of the manuscript in *favour* of the Holy Shroud of Besançon devotes folios 38 to 41 to the position of the wounds on the hands. According to him the Holy Shroud of Besançon is glorified by showing the traces of the nails in the place where painters always had placed them, and the Holy Shroud of Turin must be condemned as a forgery. In the Middle Ages—the time of rigid tradition—this fact carried greater weight than in 1700.

We give here the essential passages

" The Gospels seem to state clearly that Jesus Christ was nailed to the Cross by the palms of His hands. St. Luke says that Jesus Christ, to prove His resurrection, showed His disciples the wounds in His feet and in His hands. Now the hand cannot properly be called the wrist. In the same way Christ said to St. Thomas, ' Behold my hands.' In Psalm xxi. 18 the prophet says, ' They have pierced my hands and my feet.' It would give a forced meaning to these passages if we called hands wrists. But the words of the Prophet Zechariah would seem to decide this question altogether, ' What mean these wounds in the middle of your hands ? ' (Zech. xiii. 6). Tradition has always represented Jesus Christ fastened to the Cross by the palms of His hands, and not by the wrists; and this has been so in all places, in all times, and from the dawning of Christianity to the present century. All the Holy Fathers agree on this. All the crucifixes of the world preach the same text." Our anonymous author finally closes the discussion altogether in favour of the Holy Shroud of Besançon. We will only say this : Figure 4 gives us the backs of the hands, not the palms. There would even be nothing unreasonable in the supposition that the nails were driven in obliquely through the palms to the wrists.

The images on the Holy Shroud of Besançon are so badly executed that far from considering it to be the rival of the Shroud of Turin, it is doubtful whether it can be thought good enough even to be a copy. It *was* a copy, however, and it is important to establish this fact, as we shall see.

SKETCHES SHOWING THAT THE BESANÇON SHROUD WAS COPIED FROM THAT OF LIREY (TURIN).
Fig. 5.

In figure 5 there are three heads, A, B and C. A is a sketch from the head of Turin as it appears upon the linen cloth, executed by myself ; it is, of course, very rough, but correct in detail as far as it goes.

B has been obtained by enlarging to a similar scale a head taken from an engraving of the seventeenth century representing the Besançon Shroud. This engraving is reproduced entire in figure 6.

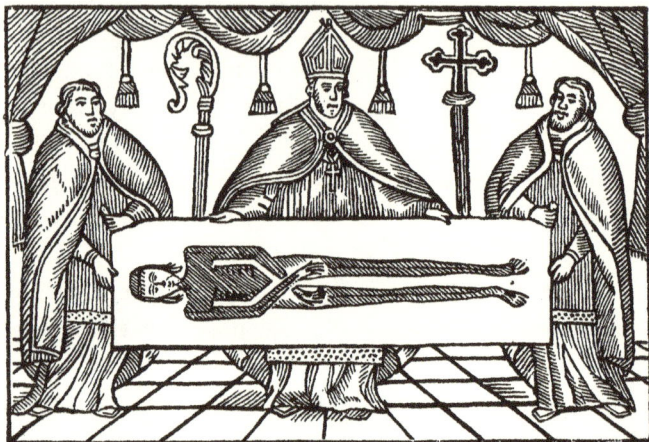

THE BESANÇON SHROUD. FROM AN ENGRAVING (XVII. CENTURY [?]).
Fig. 6.

The third head, marked C, is the similar enlargement of a photograph from one of the copies painted on linen, such as are in the possession of many of the chief families of Besançon. A photograph of this copy is shown in figure 7.

Let us now compare the three heads. Clearly the black marks correspond in all three. The salient point is the vertical line of the nose, the lower portion of which, in all three heads, grows slightly larger and inclines towards the left of the face. The engraver (more skilful than the painter on the linen), has drawn the eyebrows far apart, as in our own design. The painter, on the contrary, has merely indicated the eyebrows by a horizontal bar above the nose, and has omitted altogether to place the eyes in their sockets, which are indeed badly indicated in the original. The engraver, on the other hand, has reproduced the shape of the eye fairly well, and has designated the eyelids by a line drawn betwixt eye and brow.

Compare also the cheek-bones. In B they are omitted altogether ;

70

in C they are enormous. All the copyists of the Besançon Shroud seem to have insisted on giving them undue prominence, see Figure 7. In both B and C the oblique lines on each side of the nose, indicating the pained expression of the hollow cheeks, are clearly marked. In B indeed the engraver has endeavoured to show that the right cheek (left in the drawing) was more swollen than the opposite one.

Now note the drawing of the mouth, which is very characteristic. The engraver, B, places under the nose a large black mark, notched or irregular on the upper edge. In our own sketch this is meant for the moustache, but for the copyist it could hardly have had that signification, for it is difficult to make out even the upper lip. At any rate he gives it as he sees it. The painter, C, does much the same, indicating its droop with careful pains. Lower down, A, B and C all give a light band for the upper lip, and a dark band for the under lip. Lower still, we find another light band which shows the hollow of the chin, and separates the mouth from

COPY OF THE BESANÇON SHROUD.
Fig. 7.

the large black patch which shows the prominence of the chin itself. From the chin B and C seem to have intended to show the beard, roughly parted in the middle to indicate the two classic points, which, we may add, are little, if at all, perceptible in the Holy Shroud.

71

We think that after this examination it will be admitted that the authors of copies B and C must have worked from the original Shroud of Lirey (Turin). At any rate they have produced all the defects which we know to have been the characteristic of the Shroud of Besançon. There is no doubt, therefore, that the Shroud of Besançon was neither more nor less than a replica of that of Lirey (Turin)—a replica faithful enough in many respects as having been reverently copied, but rough and crude, because the work of unskilful hands.

To demonstrate still further. If the engraver of B and the painter of C judged it necessary to add a neck and shoulders to the figure because they thought it would have been absurd without them, they did not carry their conviction so far as to replace the absent ears. They have, however, outlined the lower jaw, which is not visible in the original.

We see in sketch A that the top of the head, on the right side of the drawing, is much stronger in tone than on the other side. Our own sketch shows that the locks of hair on that side are thicker and more marked. It is clear that B and C endeavoured at least to copy faithfully. Again, our sketch shows the thickest tress of hair curving upwards from the roots, and this curve is shown with great exactness in the sketches. In nearly all the copies of the Besançon Shroud this peculiarity is observable.

We need not say much about the rendering of the body. All the faults which the anonymous author of the manuscript found with it are here faithfully reproduced ; and this is not through any fault of the copyists, for we are given to understand clearly enough that such faults were visible in the figure on the Shroud of Besançon itself. The engraver B gives perhaps the real aspect of his model more faithfully than the artist employed by Chifflet. In any case he naïvely places on the right side the lance-wound which Chifflet has placed on the left.

We must not omit to notice the copy of the Holy Shroud, said to have been made by one Pierre Dargent, in the latter half of the sixteenth century, which we reproduce in figure 8. It is almost in the nature of an official document, as it is preserved at the present time in the library of the town of Besançon. It is also the largest copy existing.

It is a sepia drawing on linen, and we may remark, that in order to reproduce the Shroud as faithfully as possible, copies were usually made in this medium, to the exclusion of oil-colour or distemper. We know that the original Shroud of Lirey (Turin) is of a fine light fabric. The impressions, therefore, look as if stained on the cloth itself, and such an effect could only have been rendered by water-colour or sepia drawing. This particular copy is simply conceived, but is in marked contrast with others of a less sincere spirit. If the eyes and mouth are shown in positive, the nose has the appearance of being in negative, while the two cheek bones are indicated by the strangely shaped patches which are given also by the painter C in figure 4, and which were one of the striking characteristics of the Shroud of Besançon.

The sepia colouring of Pierre Dargent was used in all subsequent copies. At Besançon all the small religious pictures, painted or embroidered, are of a brown colour like sepia. We have seen many such, both in the homes of inhabitants and at the hospital of Besançon. The common stencil-plates, which reproduced holy pictures cheaply on paper were all brown in colour. Monsieur l'Abbé de Beauséjour, vicaire général de l'archevêché, showed us many of them.

To avoid confusion we must refer once more to the *Notes Iconographiques* published by Monsieur Jules Gauthier in 1883, concerning the Shroud of Besançon. At the date of publication the attention of M. Gauthier had not been drawn to certain peculiarities in the reproductions of the Shroud of which he was making a study. He did not perhaps suspect that these peculiari-

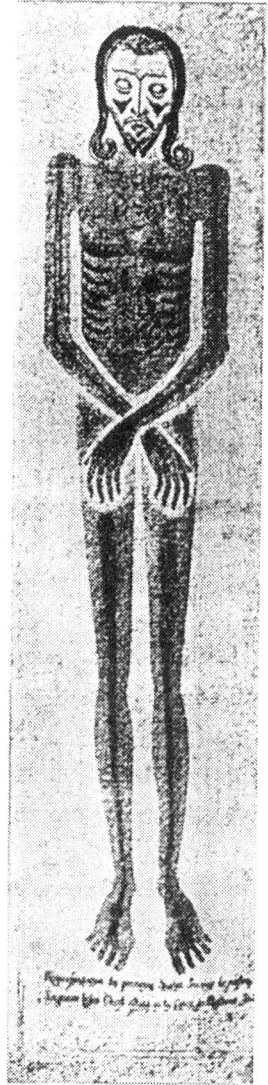

COPY OF THE BESANÇON SHROUD.
IN SEPIA BY PIERRE DARGENT
(XVI. CENTURY).
Fig. 8.

73

ties were capable of disclosing a secret. Being ignorant of the true value of the Holy Shroud of Turin, as indeed every one was until 1898, he did not realize that the Shroud of Besançon was in truth a copy thereof, and he confined his investigations to the archaeological side of the question. For this reason he attached excessive importance to the copy which he reproduces in Plate III of his work, and from which he wrongly traces the origin of all the different religious representations of the same sort, which are so numerous in that part of France. Probably he thought this copy more intelligible than the others. It is by Jean de Loisy, engraved in 1630, and is, on the contrary, one of the *least* faithful. No trace of negative representation is to be found in the features. Even the nose, which, in Chifflet's engraving, and in the painting at the Besançon library, is clearly negative, being represented in positive by de Loisy. The rendering of the body, however, corresponds with that shown in our Plate v.

Other artists of the Loisy family seemed to have made a speciality of the Besançon Shroud; one of them, Pierre, was more faithful in his work. On his Plate I., M. Gauthier gives a reproduction of this artist's work, executed in 1660. The head is here a rough negative.

To sum up : The Holy Shroud of Besançon is neither more nor less than an inferior copy of the Holy Shroud of Lirey (Turin), which must have been made between the years 1349 and 1375. Although it has no artistic merit, it is most valuable to us, being the first definite material evidence relating to the original of Turin. It proves that the image of Christ on the original Shroud was in negative long before the fire of 1532. In fact, a very short time after this painting had been executed (as alleged by its enemies) by an artist in the pay of the Charny family, it possessed unmistakably the essential characteristics which mark it to-day, characteristics which we assert destroy the theory of its having been fraudulently produced by mechanical means, pictorial or otherwise.

The Besançon Shroud also proves to us that the contemporaries of the so-called forger of Lirey were quite unaware of the real nature of the impressions which were said to have been fabricated. What indeed could they know of the values of the photographic terms, positive and negative ?

DESCRIPTIONS OF COPIES OF THE HOLY SHROUD

It seems clear that their knowledge sufficed only to produce the grotesque and ridiculous copy which we have evoked from its ashes at Besançon, and which had none of the transcendent qualities of the Holy Shroud of Turin

II

The Holy Shroud of Besançon may now, we think, be suffered to pass into oblivion. But before quitting the town in which the so-called relic was preserved up to the time of the Revolution, let us see what its historian, Dr. Chifflet, has to say; this time about the Shroud of Turin.

If, as M. Chevalier states, the Shroud of Turin was unknown to Chifflet, we must remember that he had a brother who lived at Turin, and from this fact his engravings may furnish some information, especially as Chifflet speaks of the Shroud with considerable assurance.

It was known to Chifflet that the body which had been laid in the Holy Shroud of Turin had not been washed, and he suggests that the body was covered with blood, confounding here, as many others have done, the colour of oxide of aloes with that of blood. He was aware of the clot of blood visible below the wound in the side, as well as the brown marks on the forearm. He mentions how in the Turin image the hands are shown crossed at the wrists, and he knows the position of the scourge-marks fairly well, showing them as short lines striping the upper part of the breast, the arms and back, much as they are found on the original (see our figure 4).

The conclusions which he draws are not false, although they are incomplete ; he has, in short, grasped the fact that the impressions have undergone a reversal from right to left. He has perceived that the simple act of contact did not altogether account for the impressions, and that some other special agent must have been at work for the features to have been reproduced so exactly ; but his suggestion that the Shroud must have been closely folded round the body, so closely as to be almost in the nature of a mould, only complicates the problem.

We quote the passage from his book, page 198.

" In sacrarum Imaginum coloribus, materiam specto et formam : in

THE SHROUD OF CHRIST

Taurinensi unicam materiam agnosco ; Christi cruorum, ac saniem preti-osum : in Vesontinâ praeter sanguinem, etiam ungenta." (The Besançon image was pale yellow.) " Vesontina icon extra quinque vulnera, quorum luculentus est rubor, tola ex flauo pallescit. Philippo II Hispaniarium regi cum depicta est in linteo, nullus eam color sic ementiri potuit, ut tinctura caryophyllorum et cinnamomi, per aquam vita extractae." (That of Turin was the colour of blood.) " Taurinensis Imago, ferè ubique purpureo atroque constat, nec aliud paenè quidquam nisi vulnus habet."

Concerning the hands, he says, page 189 : ". . . Sinistra iconis manus, quae dextrae Christi respondet, alteri superposita est ; tamen in Vesontino linteo carpus carpo institit ; in Taurinensi metacarpus meta-carpo. Itaque in Vesontino conspicua sunt utriusque manus vulnera ; in Taurinensi, manus altera vulnus alterius tegit." He thus describes the wounds visible on the body, page 195 : ". . . largum cruorem e manuum, pedumque, ac lateris vulneribus emissum : humeros quà flagris quà crucis gestatione conscissos afflictosque ; collum foedè in-tumescens ex funibus, catenisque, quibus vinctus ac raptatus [?] : crura, brachia, lumbos, pectus, totum corpus, vel diris ictibus contusum, vel flagellorum vibicibus confertim decussatis dissectum, vel sanguineis guttis vi verberum exussis foedè maculatum." Evidently here Chifflet attributes the entire modelling of the body to the traces of blood left by the wounds ; he was not able to understand all the markings on the Shroud.

The following sentence concerns the reversing of the images : ". . . alterum, quaecumque dextra sunt in sacris linteis, sinistra fuisse in Christi corpore ; et vicissim, hic dextra, quae illic sinistra, planè ut in speculis " (page 185).

Here is Chifflet's opinion as to the deformations which an impression by simple contact must have had : " Denique non apparet latior vultus in sacris linteis, quàm qui homini in planâ tabulâ ex arte depicto conuenit ; esset autem multo latior si ex naturali dumtaxat genarum attactu colorem contraxissit " (page 199).

We may now leave Besançon and betake ourselves to Chambéry.

DESCRIPTIONS OF COPIES OF THE HOLY SHROUD

First of all here is the actual account of the repairs made in the cloth two years after the fire of 1534, when the Holy Shroud was nearly destroyed. The account is given by the nuns of St. Claire, who had been commissioned by the Duke of Savoy to undertake such repairs and consolidations as were deemed indispensable. These ladies were at work on the Shroud for fifteen days, and they describe it most minutely in *Le Saint Suaire de Chambéry à Sainte-Claire-en-Ville* (April to May, 1534), by L. Bouchage. Chambéry, Drivet, 1891.

It was on April 15, 1534, that the Cardinal Louis de Gorrevod proceeded to make an official inspection of the Holy Shroud. Bouchage gives us the account of the ceremony, and, more interesting still, the precise terms in which the Cardinal describes the fire and the traces left by it on the Shroud, just as they are visible to-day. " Licet in duobus plicis a dextris et a sinistris appareat in duodecim locis ex dicto incendio certa angredo, et in aliquo dictorum locorum ex dicto incendio aliqualis debilitatio et in ipsa nigredine fractura, extra tamen effigiem et impressionem Sudoris et Sanguinis Corporis Christi."

After this ceremony, according to Piano (who translated Bouchage, and who himself made a study of early history), the Shroud was taken to the Monastery of Saint Claire. Piano states that Chifflet preserved the names of the nuns to whom specially the repairing of the Shroud was entrusted. He alludes further to an account of the incident, which had been lost, but which was said to have been written by the nuns in a simple and natural style. Of this account M. Bouchage discovered a copy dating from the last century, and this copy may be deemed authentic, as " bearing the names of the same persons as cited by Piano, such as Pingin, Chifflet and Capré, but with more numerous and precise details" (page 12). We must add, and this is a noteworthy fact, that the writer of this account (a nun) had been an eye-witness of the repairs to the Holy Shroud, and had personally and with much care inspected the impressions on it.

The nun who gives the account mentions, first of all, the solemn official report which was made of the actual delivery of the Shroud into the hands of the Abbess Louise de Vargin. The papal legate requested the noblemen present to examine the relic minutely, and to bear witness that it was the actual winding-sheet which had been venerated previous to the fire. After this the narrator goes on to tell how the Holy Shroud was carefully backed with a piece of Holland cloth, and pieces were sewn on to repair the holes burnt by the fire. As they worked the nuns remarked that the sacred impressions were nearly as visible on the back as on the front of the Shroud. Since 1534, however, the lining thus added has of course prevented any inspection of the back.

The Clarisses (as the nuns of St. Claire of Chambéry were called) noticed the trickles of blood which had stained the forehead, and the narrator makes special mention of a large drop over the left eyebrow. " We noticed," she says, " on the left side of the forehead a drop of blood larger and longer than the others—' elle serpente en onde ' " (p. 20, M. Bouchage). This is very important, as being the only testimony we have concerning this truly remarkable trace. They understood that the figures were of the nature of impressions, and they indicate as clearly as possible that they considered the impression to be a species of modelling. " The eyebrows appeared well defined ; the eyes a little less clear ; the nose as being the most prominent part of the face was well marked " ; the form of the mouth and the swollen condition of the parts of the face were also noticed. " The mouth was well shown, small but finely shaped ; the cheeks were swollen and disfigured as if they bore the cruel marks of blows, more particularly on the right side of the face."

They mention the trickles of blood on the forearms and the marks of the nails in the *middle* of the hand. The narrator must have made a mistake here, as we know by ocular demonstration that the marks of the nails are in the wrists. The wound on the side is described as being " three fingers long."

In dealing with the back view of the body mention is made of the hair being clotted with blood, and the narrator specially mentions what is perfectly exact, that the clots are heavier on the nape of the neck than on the hair higher up. " On the head there are the marks of long, sharp thorns, so closely set together that the crown of thorns must evidently have fitted almost like a hat, and not like a prince's crown as represented in pictures ; on close examination it can be seen that the wounds were more severe towards the back of the head near its nape, and that the thorns had here penetrated deeper, by the largeness of the drops of blood with which the hair is matted together " (p. 21). It was noticed that " the shoulders were entirely lacerated and torn by scourge-marks extending over the whole body." No mention, however, is made of the heavy bruise which is to be found between the shoulder and the right shoulder-blade, caused by the terrible pressure of the Cross. On parts of the back " the drops of blood are as large as the leaves of marjoram, and the skin is broken in many places by the savage blows inflicted."

We must point out some errors in this account. The body was not, as the nuns believed, so closely covered with wounds ; the impressions were not produced by blood in a liquid state. No vestige is to be seen of the iron chain by which the body might have been bound ; we shall explain this further on. But such slight errors do not detract in any way from the value of the testimony given by " the poor Claires " of 1534.

At Chambéry, in the chapel of the Castle, is a recent painting in water-colour (brown monochrome) on a canvas of the same size as the original Shroud, but it is too roughly executed to be of any value to us. By the kindness of M. de Buttel we were allowed to see a smaller copy preserved in the church of Notre Dame. It is very ancient, probably dating from the sixteenth century, and we have had it photographed, and reproduced in Plate IX.

This also is a brown monochrome in water-colour, and is the most complete copy we know. In spite of its evident imperfections, its testimony is very valuable. Round the eyes, the nose, and the mouth are those light zones which indicate negative modelling. We remark that no neck is visible. The wound from the nails is clearly shown in the wrist, and blood is seen on the forearms. Under the heels the artist has shown marks of blood, but by force of tradition he has thought fit to place the stigmata in the soles of the feet. In the actual Shroud all the blood-marks on the feet are alike except those under the heels, which are larger, and it is here that blood has flowed directly upon the linen. The copyist, having placed the *stigmata* in the centres of the soles of the feet, has been obliged to mark them on the upper part, which corresponded ; and, as we shall see further on, he has placed these markings too low down.

The artist has lessened the general value of the picture by making a multitude of fine lines all over the body. He has done this from a false interpretation, believing, like Chifflet, and like the " Clarisses " of 1534, that the image had been produced by liquid blood, and therefore making the wound-marks as he thought they must have been. In so doing he gives the scourge-marks as they would have been inflicted by flexible rods capable of cutting, not bruising, the skin, as the Roman flagella does.

We now pass to Italy, for there is to be found the very remarkable miniature painting by Giulio Clovio, which we have reproduced in this work as our frontispiece. Our readers will have seen for themselves how the power and imagination of the artist are diminished when he has to paint an object the exact signification of which is not clear to his own mind. Who indeed in the sixteenth century, or at any other time, could have guessed that the very faults in the moulding of the contours, the absence of precision in the outlines of the sacred impressions, are the scientific basis on which our argument rests ? Who indeed could have had the strength of mind to confine himself to the reproduction of what seemed to be evidently faults in design ?

We are indebted to M. le barron A. Manno and to M. Chevalier Secondo Pia for an excellent photographic proof of another miniature, painted on silk, and preserved likewise in the Pinacothek at Turin. It also dates from the sixteenth century, and these gentlemen incline to think that probably it also is the work of Giulio Clovio. However this may be, the angels holding up the Holy Shroud are painted in the same manner as those shown in our frontispiece, but the impressions on the Shroud itself are somewhat differently treated. The general sweep of the body is more thick-set, and the features more in detail. Their rendering is entirely negative. We cannot, however, go so far as to say that we find in the photographic proof from this miniature the full expression of the original.

Both miniatures have a sort of *perizoma* exactly like that on the Chambéry drawing. Their painters, however, have not gone so far as to invent a knotting of the cloth, as the engraver of Chifflet's plate has done ; they have only given additional force to certain light-coloured bands which, across the image on the Holy Shroud, mark the rise of the loins or express the hollows situated between the legs and the fleshy parts of the pelvis.

We may glean some further useful details from other Italian copies. There is one, an engraving of which has been shown us by M. de Buttel.

This was done at the time of the journey undertaken by Carlo Borromeo, archbishop of Milan, when he came to Turin in 1578 to do reverence to the Holy Shroud. We cannot learn much from the modelling of the body, which in many respects is incorrect, but it shows clearly the marks of the nails, the wounds being in the wrists and near the ankles.

Another copy on linen was executed in 1650. It is the same size as the original, and is in the possession of Count Ernest Gay de Montoriolo—handed down from the Counts Salpone, who held high office in the royal household. It is a roughly painted water-colour, remarkable chiefly for the fact that the nose and eyes are distinctly painted as negative. The wounds of the nails are shown in the wrists and near the ankles.

So, then, two copies made from the Holy Shroud show the wounds in the feet near the ankles. It is evident, we think, that the painters of these copies have placed the wounds a little too high up. In his photograph M. Pia has reproduced the front of the figure as far down as the ankles, but not far enough down to distinguish the nail-marks near the ankles. Nevertheless we believe that these wounds on the feet were not as traditionally indicated, in the middle of the sole. We already know that under the feet the largest clots are near the heels, and by combining this observation with the indications afforded by the Italian copyists we judge that the nails were driven in at the junction of the tarsal and metatarsal bones. The wounds in the feet in the front aspect of the figure would thus be situated at a spot analogous to where M. Pia shows the wound in the left hand. Not until we are able to examine the Holy Shroud itself can this detail be definitely settled.

Before leaving Italy we may say a few words about a miniature on parchment which has been submitted to our inspection. It bears the date 1559, probably incorrectly ; but some writing on the back has enabled M. Paul Meyer, Member of the Institute and Keeper of the Records, to fix its date about the seventeenth century. The face is roughly drawn in as negative. The painter has somewhat naïvely mistaken the side-locks of hair for linen folds ; the wound in the side, placed correctly, is shown as a species of rosette which supports the linen swathings. There is no neck. The miniature is executed in some brown tint. Its general aspect reminds one of Clovio's work, of which it may be a copy.

In Spain there exists, in the Monastery of Silos, a copy of the Holy Shroud, of full original size, dating without doubt from the seventeenth century. It shows an enormous perizoma, and its drawing cannot be called faithful. However, this detail may be noted by its rarity ; the scourge marks on the thighs and calves are closely reproduced. The blows are accurately shown in the shape of small narrow rectangular lines.

In Portugal, at Xabregas, a suburb of Lisbon, there is another copy of the Shroud. Full particulars of this are given in the *History of the Holy Shroud*, by M. de Mély, which appeared in the *Revue Archéologique* in 1902. The first mention of this Shroud is in a work 1651–57. The author does not seek to maintain that it is the original. In 1709 another author put forward the theory that the Shroud at the Monastery of Xabregas might really be the original Shroud. Here follows an allusion to a so-called miraculous reproduction of the Shroud at Turin, not the handiwork of any painter. This might be the wonderful tracing which we found at Lisbon, unless indeed we admit the hypothesis that it was the primitive original ! The two Shrouds, the old one and the new, were so alike, says an author of 1709, that it was impossible to distinguish the one from the other.

The truth is that the Shroud of Xabregas is a copy of the Holy Shroud of Turin—nearly as faithful a copy as the one which we have reproduced in our Plate IX.

M. de Mély having been so good as to show us the photographs of the Lisbon Shroud, we were able to point out to him all the traces of negative modelling which were visible on the inferior painting of Xabregas. We also showed him that the artist had interpreted the marks which run across the loins in the original of Turin to be an actual chain. We have already pointed out that this stain, which has been taken by so many people to be the marks of the chain by which Jesus Christ was bound to the flogging-post, was the water-stain made at the time of the fire. Also the feet are not drawn faithfully. They are shown crossed, the one over the other, instead of being stretched out side by side in normal fashion. Compare our figure 33, reproducing the Calvary of Taddeo Gaddi.

Finally, let us return to France, to direct attention to a somewhat fantastically executed engraving of the seventeenth century. We see in this what liberties copyists allowed themselves to take with the reality. This engraving is so well known that we need only say that, except in the general position of the two bodies, it has hardly any connexion with the original. It bears no trace of negative treatment ; indeed we might almost think we were gazing upon a picture of some statue, executed in the style of the time of Louis XIV.

The evidence afforded by the various copies and descriptions of the Holy Shroud is of considerable value. The relic is, as it were, authenticated in almost all important details ; so much so, that our knowledge of the subject thus gleaned is almost equal to what was afforded to us by the photographs taken from the original.

But let us not forget that these copyists, these observers, could after all only convey to us what they themselves knew. The eye indeed will only perceive what the mind comprehends, or nearly so, and whoever wishes to accumulate precise facts must do so by close comparison of details. Admitting, then, that by a stroke of good fortune we had discovered one single copy of the Holy Shroud which united in itself all the peculiarities which we have thus laboriously collected from so many sources, even then, such a copy could but have been the shadow, of the original Shroud. We should have obtained from it no fruitful knowledge, because the negative image, though materially complete in appearance, could not have been otherwise than inexact, inartistic, and unscientific in important details. Consequently even the ideal copyist, whom we have vainly sought, at Besançon, at Chambéry, and Turin, would have been powerless to *reproduce* the original Shroud ; how much more powerless to create it.

CHAPTER V

THE FACE ON THE HOLY SHROUD, COMPARED WITH IMAGINATIVE PORTRAITS

THE impressions on the Shroud of Christ, which are of so much interest to all students of science, have yet another even wider interest, inasmuch as when the imprints undergo photographic reversion, they reveal as we claim the very features of the Saviour Himself. It is in fact the only real portrait existing of the Christ, and therefore is in no way comparable with the imaginary works, no matter how beautiful or how highly renowned, of bygone sculptors and painters.

It is, however, well worth while to review very shortly the various impressions formed in the past of the appearance of Jesus Christ and to consider how much or how little they resemble the actual portrait as revealed by the Holy Shroud.

It would, of course, far exceed the limits of this work to enter into any detailed examination of all the known portraits of Christ. Every artist has considered himself free to treat the sacred features according to his own feeling and imagination ; nevertheless, with a few exceptions, a certain normal type has been maintained, so much so that in gazing at the Holy Shroud we might almost believe that the face here revealed is the archetype on which the world's portraiture has been based. A noble and majestic countenance, the face long and oval, the nose slightly aquiline, the mouth small and well shaped, the beard of moderate length, while the hair, parted in the centre, falls in long locks upon the shoulders. Such is, in truth, the traditional appearance of the Christ as known and exemplified in art. But in this head are also visible such mingled power and sweetness, such depth of suffering conquered, such nobility of peace attained, that as we gaze our hearts are filled with reverence and awe.

THE FACE ON THE HOLY SHROUD

The image of Turin bears the mark of no special epoch. For the art critic, as well as for the man of science, it is simply a direct natural representation. If it had been the work of an artist it would have been more correct—the outlines would have been more exact, the contours better defined. Neck and ears would probably have been added, and the shoulders made clearer. The nostrils, the eyes, and the beard would have been more exactly defined. Nor can we believe that an artist living centuries ago would have been content with those poor meshes of hair clotted with blood and sweat.

Is it to the hand of a painter in the pay of some feudal lord, or to the laborious monk member of some arid fraternity that we can attribute the serene majesty which characterizes the features of our Lord on the Shroud of Turin ? How could such a task have been performed without vulgarity ? What imagination, what genius would be required to evoke from the dim shades of antiquity this shadowy but awful form ?

Greek art at its best period was either religious or heroic ; it expressed with perfect nobility of sentiment the serenity and majesty of the gods and heroes of ancient mythology.

By degrees its expression became more human, more formal, and indeed more sensual. We find, however, certain portrait busts of philosophers and poets in which high moral and mental development are powerfully expressed.

If the Greek sculptors had been dealing with the Christ ideal they would doubtless have produced a head as complete and grand as that of the well known Aesculapius ; they would have realized in marble the great miracle-worker, a priest or prophet of God, but they could not have shown us " the Good Shepherd," who cures the body only in order to touch the soul; and they would have had no sympathy for the voluntary victim, humble and lowly, expiating the faults of others. There is no renunciation of self in Greek philosophy. In short, no figure in Greek art is comparable to that of Christ.

We need not refer to the Bacchus in the National collection at Naples, but in the same collection we find a fine head (fig. 9), the Farnese Neptune, which would equally well represent Jupiter. This bust lives ; the

THE SHROUD OF CHRIST

mouth—the whole impression—commands. It is indeed one of the immortals, but it possesses none of the Divine pity of the Christ ; it wots not, cares not for the sufferings of humanity. Note how in this bust the workmanship is clear, distinct, and powerful ; every chisel-mark tells.

If not among the gods of antiquity, is it among the thinkers of antiquity that we shall recognize the type of the Christ ?

We do not think that the beautiful bronze head at Naples is a Plato; it might as well be a bearded Bacchus. But there are some busts which

THE FARNESE NEPTUNE (NAPLES MUSEUM).
Fig. 9.

AESCHINUS (NAPLES MUSEUM).
Fig. 10.

may be actual portraits—the Sophocles in the Musée de Latéran at Rome, the Demosthenes of the Vatican, the Aeschinus of Naples.

The bust of Sophocles—admitting, that is to say, that it is Sophocles— shows us a handsome man, sure of himself, and conscious of his powers. He folds himself majestically in his toga.

Both the Demosthenes and the Aeschinus are admirable as works of art ; both are instinct with the knowledge of life, both bear the marks of profound meditation. The Aeschinus is distinctly antique in type ; the

86

head of Demosthenes (fig. 11) is, in comparison, modern.   They are both sad faces, softened by the experience of suffering, gazing as it were at human misery, wishful to help, to console, men perhaps of the noblest type, but after all mere men ; and it is from no mortal head that we can seek the type of the Saviour of mankind.   The head upon the Holy Shroud, though dead, seems still to be gazing higher, and still higher, through the closed, still eyelids.

It is known that the early Christians, in the mural and sepulchral pictures of the Catacombs, made no effort to portray the Saviour.   The figure of the Good Shepherd, which is found there, young and beardless, bearing on his shoulders the lost sheep, is not a portrait but a symbol.   Indeed, among all the discoveries of mural decoration, or sepulchral ornament found in the Catacombs there is nothing of any real artistic merit.   The first and earliest representations of Christ are of an Oriental character.   Nowhere in classic art is to be found any trace of the Byzantine type of Christ.   To find this type of countenance which for so many centuries prevailed in art, we must leave Rome and Athens and seek for the Semitic

DEMOSTHENES (VATICAN MUSEUM).
Fig. 11.

prototype in Syria.   The examination of this later Greek art is the more interesting as the lineaments of the body impressed on the Holy Shroud are undoubtedly those of a man of Oriental race.   The Byzantine Christs have a certain air of resemblance, but have nevertheless essential individual differences.

We give here three examples, which will be sufficient to indicate the character of this epoch.   At the same time we reproduce one of those ancient Graeco-Egyptian portraits, which have been discovered in the tombs

87

PORTRAIT OF A SYRO-PHŒNICIAN NOBLE
(THEODORE GRAF COLLECTION).
Fig. 12.

of Upper Egypt. The one given here (fig. 12) is from the interesting collection of M. Theodore Graf, of Vienna.

This portrait, when compared with that of the Christ of Ravenna, shows the influence of the Semitic type on Byzantine art. The two types are in fact almost identical. The forehead is low, the eyebrows well arched, the nose long and straight, slightly rounded at the lower extremity ; the mouths, with their heavy lips and the symmetrical oval of the faces, are almost identical in both portraits. The hair, beard, and general expression are differently treated. The Graeco-Egyptian painter has more talent than the Christian worker in mosaic.

The vague and slightly astonished expression of the Ravenna Christ (fig. 13) contrasts disadvantageously with that of the Syro-Phoenician nobleman, who has the air of one who knows his own rank. The excessive largeness of the eyes in this last might be thought due to an exaggeration of the artist, but it

THE RAVENNA CHRIST (VI. CENTURY).
Fig. 13.

must be remembered that by imme-
morial custom, existing in Egypt to
the present time, it is usual to give
expression to the eyes by painting a
dark circle round them. It will be
seen from the foregoing remarks, and
from a comparison of the pictures, that
the Ravenna Christ is the work of an
artist who has adopted and adapted
a previously well known type. He is
quite uninspired and has not known
how to transfuse into his work either
the soul of an apostle or the exaltation
of the martyr. At Palermo, in the
Church of La Martorana, and in the
Palatine Chapel, are to be found two

THE MARTORANA CHRIST, PALERMO
(XII. CENTURY).
Fig. 14.

representations of Christ (figs. 14 and 15) attributed to artists of the
twelfth century, which in ethnical type are greatly superior to that of
Ravenna ; the eyes have not the same vagueness, the lips are more re-

CHRIST. THE PALATINE CHAPEL, PALERMO
(XII. CENTURY)
Fig. 15.

fined, the Semitic contours are
modified. It is apparent that
the figure on the Holy Shroud
shares in many respects the
race - characteristics of these
heads, without being precisely
the same.

Having made this admis-
sion, however, it is impossible
to deny the overpowering su-
periority, from an artistic point
of view, of the portrait on the
Holy Shroud. Being an imprint
from nature, the contrast between it and the priestly con-

89

CHRIST. CLUNY MUSEUM
(XII. CENTURY).
Fig. 16.

ception of the Byzantine pictures is accentuated. There can indeed be no question of finding any trace of Byzantine art in the Shroud; where is there any treatment of feature? Where is the symmetrical oval of the face, or the hair so neatly and correctly divided over the exact middle of the forehead, or the little supplementary curl which shows itself at the parting. There is in the Byzantine pictures a symmetrical rigidity not without a certain grandeur, but in the Shroud the awful sublimity shines forth as from a living man, and the features, although stilled by death, have preserved their majesty.

And now that we know the Oriental origin of the man whose body was wrapped in the Holy Shroud of Turin, let us turn our attention again westward.

After a blank period of more than eight hundred years we find a fresh beginning, as it were, of sacred art—but only a beginning. The Christ of Vezelay, for instance, is still altogether an archaic production. The head is uninteresting, and the body disproportionately long. Much the same may be said of the Cluny Christ, here reproduced (fig. 16). The statue of

CHRIST. CHARTRES CATHEDRAL
(XII. CENTURY).
Fig. 17.

90

THE FACE ON THE HOLY SHROUD

Christ which adorns the middle door on the west front of Chartres Cathedral (fig. 17) shows progress, but we cannot regard it as anything but immature work. Both these are twelfth century.

The thirteenth century, as is well known, marks the highest point of the first French Renaissance, which already in the fourteenth century began to decline. It was a period when some admirable works were produced. We may cite the statues of St. Firmin at Amiens and that of St. Theodore at Chartres, not to mention the famous Eve of Rheims, that disturbing woman who carries in her arms the evil spirit incarnate in the shape of a salamander, and who is hesitating whether or not to take the apple that the beast holds in its jaws. One may admire at Cluny the draped statue which came from the Sainte Chapelle at Paris ; it is almost a perfect example.

All, however, are not equally beautiful. The *Christ in the act of blessing* at Vezelay looks at His visitors with a tranquil air, the eyes somewhat prominent, and the figure leaning a little in a quasi-familiar attitude. The mouth, however, is full of expression. A breath of true art like this elevates in our eyes the artists of the thirteenth century, who, whatever their faults, were never either awkward or cold. Better still, we may draw attention to the *Christ teaching* (fig. 18) on the south door of Chartres Cathedral. This is a life-like presentment. It is a teacher persuasive and persuaded, but none the less it is but a man, an ordinary French artizan, such as one might meet anywhere in the town and in whom no ray of inspiration can be perceived.

CHRIST TEACHING.
CHARTRES CATHEDRAL
(XIII. CENTURY).
Fig. 18.

Of thirteenth century work, however, the classic Christ is undoubtedly the " *Beau Dieu* " of Amiens (fig. 19). This is the work most admired by M. le Chanoine Chevalier, although he is wrong in comparing it with the Christ of the Holy Shroud. Certainly it is most beautiful—not indeed the beauty of the Grecian type, nor even is it perhaps beautiful in form, but the calm serenity of its expression is of infinite beauty.

We have alluded previously to the haughty impassiveness of the Farnese Neptune regardless of humanity on his Olympian heights, and there is perhaps some of this god-like indifference in the vague, fixed, far-away look of the " *Beau Dieu* " of Amiens. There is no pride in this look ; it is the

LE BEAU DIEU. AMIENS CATHEDRAL (XIII. CENTURY).
Fig. 19.

face of one detached, of one who has not known, or has at least forgotten, the very names even of our poor human passions, and who would never sacrifice himself in order to teach us the glorious lessons of suffering.

The chief characteristic of this beautiful head, then, is its impassiveness, but this is no quality of the true Christ. Do we not remember the timid gesture of the woman in the Gospels, who hardly dared to touch the mantle of the Saviour, though He, the Consoler, knew and felt at once what was passing in her heart ? Consider the mouth of the " *Beau Dieu.*"

92

THE FACE ON THE HOLY SHROUD

From such a mouth could come words of an exquisite purity it is true, but not great Truths. It is not the mouth of a master or of a prophet, and in this beautiful head we search vainly for one touch of Divine inspiration, one breath of the Deity.

We think, then, that between the Christ of the Holy Shroud and the "*Beau Dieu*" of Amiens there is no identity of spirit ; but besides this there is all the difference between the vague mystical expression of the one and the unmistakable look of agony suffered in the other. The dead face of Lirey shows the suffering of the flesh ; the Amiens head is a beautifully sculptured block of marble— marble which has neither bones to break, nerves to suffer, nor blood to shed.

Moreover, between the two figures there is no tie of race. There can be no doubt when we look on the Amiens head, with its straight nose slightly tilted at the tip and sharply cut, that it has been modelled from a man of Northern France. The mouth itself is purely Western in type, the eyebrows also, though they have a touch of mysticism, may be seen among the Flemish people of to-day. The beard is in purely French style ; the like may be met with in the streets of Bourges. There is nothing in all these features to indicate any Semitic or Eastern origin. In a word, the head of Amiens, beautiful as it undoubtedly is, must be considered as the very last in which to find any resemblance to the Divine face imprinted on the Holy Shroud.

To complete the artistic tradition which has inspired the author of the Amiens head we must compare it with other statues of a like place and period. Let us take the figure of Christ, which stands over the central entrance of Bourges Cathedral (fig. 20), not the ancient figure on the tympanum, but the more spirited and so to speak elegant one which stands on the pillar separating the two doors. This also is a

CHRIST TEACHING.
BOURGES CATHEDRAL
(XIII. CENTURY).
Fig. 20.

93

"Christ teaching," but it is only an inferior copy of the "*Beau Dieu*";
the drapery is treated in the same way, only it is a little less natural and
happy in general execution.   The head has not the same beauty, it is more
emaciated, and perhaps not quite anatomically correct ; but the main
features of detail—the eyebrows, the eyes, the nose—are the same.   The
mouth is of the Amiens type, but grosser and more common.   The hair and
beard are alike in both examples ; specially we may notice the mous-
taches, which, somewhat thin and drooping, curve inwards not very grace-
fully.   The thick curls of the beard in both statues take exactly the same
somewhat heavy and formal contours.

Look now upon the Divine face in the Holy Shroud ; it is nature
itself.

In this short sketch of the different representations of Christ, dating
about the thirteenth century, we have only alluded to the head, because in
all the statues and pictures mentioned the body is covered with drapery.
It seems clear that no artist of that date has produced anything that can
compare in natural truth of form and beauty with the image on the Shroud
of Turin.

If, then, the Christ of the Holy Shroud is found to be so incom-
parably superior to the representations of the thirteenth century, it com-
pares even more favourably with those of the century following—works
which are often beautiful but unequal in execution, and often attain only

AN APOSTLE.
CLUNY MUSEUM
(XIV. CENTURY).
Fig. 21.

to mediocrity in artistic ideal.   It is sufficient to
refer to a few of the best known examples ; for
instance, the statue of an apostle belonging formerly to the ancient Church of St. Jacques, but
now preserved in the Cluny collection (fig. 21).
We reproduce this merely in contrast to the severe religious austerity which characterized the
work of the previous century, and to show the
kind of art which was produced in the north of
France at the time that the Charny family founded
the Abbey of Lirey.   The art of the fourteenth century was weaker, languid, and more affected.

Sometimes it descended even to vulgar ugliness. At Notre Dame de Paris, for instance, in the choir screen there are scenes from the life of Christ, sculptured and painted ; those on the right can be well seen in the afternoon light. We give here as an example of this work the figure of Christ when He was mistaken by Mary Magdalen for the gardener (fig. 22). This series of scenes may well be considered as the work of the best artists of the period, and they are curious and interesting as studies, but altogether wanting in depth of thought or nobility of design. It is not that the artist has made the figure of Christ vulgar only by placing a spade in its hand ; it is by the want of proportion in the head, which is too big for the body, by the shortness of the commonplace nose, the heavy brows, the obstinate expression, all conveying poverty of detail, a characteristic indeed which pervades the whole work.

CHRIST AS THE GARDENER.
NOTRE DAME, PARIS
(XIV. CENTURY).
Fig. 22.

Further examples of the decadence of the period are not wanting. Let us take the group (here reproduced) where St. Thomas touches the wound in the Saviour's side (fig. 23). The original is to be found in the Cathedral of Semur in the ancient province of Burgundy. It may be urged that the level of art in so remote a locality could not be expected to rise to the height of the capital; but, on the other hand, was the town of Troyes, near which the abbey of Lirey was found, any less provincial than Semur ? The man who chiselled the head of St. Thomas was no novice ; but can the name of artist be given to him who conceived in his mind the type here given of the Christ ?

It is clear, then, that the contemporaries of the supposititious forger of Lirey were not men of any lofty artistic ideals, as shown at either Paris or Semur. In a wooden bust of Christ attributed to the fourteenth century,

CHRIST AND ST. THOMAS. SEMUR EN AUXOIS (XIV. CENTURY).
Fig. 23.

which is to be found at Pontoise (fig. 24), we rise, however, to a slightly higher level. Here at least is a sincere attempt on the part of the artist to represent the Christ in His true ethnical type, and we realize that in so doing he has had to break with the traditions of his time. The long aquiline nose of the Christ of Pontoise is entirely different from that of the *Beau Dieu* of Amiens or of the apostle of the church of St. Jacques. Here, then, at least is a man who means to plough his own furrow. What is the result of his efforts?

Alas! the head is in no way striking, for without laying stress on the poverty of design shown in the brow and mouth, the eyes, cast down,

HEAD OF CHRIST CARVED IN WOOD AT PONTOISE (XIV. CENTURY).
Fig. 24.

show no indication of intelligence, love, or pity. Such a Christ as this could inspire no respect, no veneration. The formal awkwardness of the head proves moreover that the sculptor was by no means master of his craft.

It may be thought that to strengthen our argument we are purposely bringing forward the commoner class of works, but this is not so.

In the second half of the fourteenth century, there lived an artist of really high renown, André Beauneveu of Valenciennes. To arrive at a just appreciation of this artist we have only the statue by him of Charles V at Saint Denis, and the reproductions of some miniatures of his which are given by Monsieur P. Durrieu in his interesting review of this artist's work. The recumbent statue of Charles V is in truth very fine ; it is indeed of the nature of an actual portrait : but many a master could produce a striking likeness when working directly from life, who would fail, when drawing only by his imagination. In a miniature which adorns the *Très Belles Heures du duc de Berry* we find this to be the case. The portrait of Charles V seen in profile occupies the foreground. This portrait is excellent in every way, but behind the King are the figures of two of the Saints, and these, alas ! are executed in a very inferior manner. How awkward the drawing of the nose and mouth in the St. John the Baptist ! The feet are almost ridiculous, and the same may be said of the hands of St. Andrew.

When M. Durrieu goes on to attribute to Beauneveu *Les Petites Heures du duc de Berry* (an assumption which we are not prepared altogether to endorse), it cannot be denied that in one of the miniatures representing the Trinity the two heads representing God the Father and God the Son are sadly wanting in expression ; indeed it might almost seem that they are modelled on the same lines as the unpleasing heads of St. John the Baptist and St. Andrew, to which we have just referred.

In the first half year of the *Gazette des Beaux Arts* for 1898 there are two articles by Monsieur A. de Champeaux treating historically of all the ancient schools of Burgundian and Flemish painters, and it must be confessed that the treatment of the figure of Christ as conceived by these ancient masters is anything but attractive. We may specially call attention to a dead Christ, supported by God the Father, by Malouel (about 1400), and to another of Christ on the Cross by Henri de Bellechose (about 1415) : both are neither more nor less than ugly.

To sum up, then : neither to André Beauneveu, nor to any other sculptor or painter of like ability, can we attribute the artistic breadth and vigour, far less, the nobility of conception, so wonderfully expressed in the Holy Shroud.

We should have given an incomplete idea of what could be done by the art of the fourteenth century if we were to limit our outlook to France alone. The first French Renaissance does not, it is true, seem to us worthy of such a task as the production of the Holy Shroud, but let us consider the claims of the great Italian masters, such as Giotto, Duccio, and others. We may call to mind the *Calvary* of the Upper Church of Assisi, of which in Plate VI. we have reproduced a curious fragment. Can the author thereof have been Cimabue ? We think not ; that would be to increase its age by half a century. The fresco is much deteriorated by time, and, having turned negative for the most part, it is somewhat difficult to decipher. A whole legion of angels are flying round a Christ of supernatural size ; the grouping and flight of this angelic host is well rendered. Unfortunately, however, the features of the Christ Himself are barely distinguishable, and in this much, our examination must be incomplete. The ability of the artist, however, to produce beautiful and energetic heads cannot be denied, for in the group to the left, the enemies of Christ, there are some remarkable heads, as may be seen in the facsimile we give. But even these heads are so rough in execution, that we see how impossible it would have been for the painter to execute a face with the delicacy and nobility of expression which such a task would demand.

Giotto was doubtless a contemporary of the unknown author of the Assisi fresco, and we know that for picturesque grouping and general movement, his work is excellent. But the Christs painted by him are uniformly uninteresting, whether we consider the heads only, or the general treatment. There is at Padua a fresco of *Christ raising Lazarus*, which has been photographed ; the outlines are badly drawn, but the grouping and general movement are well rendered.

THE FACE ON THE HOLY SHROUD

From our point of view, the two most instructive works of Giotto are *The Descent from the Cross* and *The Entombment*, both in the Lower Church at Assisi. In a general way the qualities and defects of these two works are much the same as in the fresco of Padua ; above all, we recognize the puny imagination of the artist when he attempts to depict the body of Christ borne by the reverent hands of the disciples to the sepulchre. It is a difficult subject, but we may add that in the many heads of Christ executed by this artist the work is usually bad.

As a parallel to *The Calvary* of Assisi we should wish to put a work by Duccio di Buoninsegna on the same subject, which is at Sienna. Here we shall see that art has made rapid progress. The group of Pharisees is painted with singular force, but as soon as spirituality of expression is necessary the power of the artist diminishes, and we find the holy women and the friends of Christ only moderately conceived, while the figure of the Christ Himself is without strength—without beauty—it leaves us cold.

At Assisi also is to be found some of the work of Taddeo Gaddi, an energetic but unequal artist a few years younger than Giotto. We reproduce here his *Calvary* (fig. 25), if it be but to show that the task was greater than he was able to perform. The composition gives just the three essential figures, the Christ, the Virgin, and St. John, a proof that the artist desires to concentrate his powers of imagination and technique. Some parts of the work are in fact quite admirable. The Saint John is most powerful ; never has painting, even at its best, given a more sincere and dramatic attitude, or more expressive line of drapery—the head in its agony of entreaty is inexpressibly grand. The figure of the Virgin, however, is, we think, less powerfully conceived ; the expression of sorrow is almost a grimace. But let us consider the central figure, the Christ. Here it is that the artist's lack of power is conspicuous ; the head might have been hewed out with a hatchet, and the rendering of the body, while aspiring to truth, is really little else than vulgar. No doubt Taddeo Gaddi wished to emphasize the anatomy of the figure—to show the muscles, the veins, and the distortion of the feet violently drawn together—but the effect is repulsive.

THE SHROUD OF CHRIST

With the painters Giotto and Duccio we were conscious of an effort to idealize—to draw from the inward vision a touching and spiritual representation—but in Taddeo Gaddi we have also a honest conscientious worker, who in his endeavour to paint naturally, sinks to the level of mere realism.

CALVARY. BY TADDEO GADDI AT ASSISI (XIV. CENTURY).
Fig. 25.

But at this very period, at this epoch in the history of the world's Art, the Christ on the Shroud shows neither weakness nor brutality.

Thus we pass beyond the fateful date of 1353. The suppositious author of the figure on the Shroud has been vainly sought in France, while in Italy we have found no work of that period which could rank as its artistic equal. We may now usefully glance at the subsequent centuries and their productions.

THE FACE ON THE HOLY SHROUD

In France we may mention the *Enshrouding of Christ* at the Abbey of Solesme. It is an important piece of fifteenth century work, a model of which may be seen at the Trocadero. Many portions of it are very good ; the body of the recumbent Christ is a fine piece of modelling, but the head is cold and lacks expression. A somewhat similar subject is *The Entomb-ment* of Saint Mihiel at the Church of St. Stephen, a sixteenth-century group by Ligier-Richard. A cast of this is also to be found at the Museum of Comparative Sculpture. The artist is a perfect master of technicality, but the figure of Christ is heavily done—a large, unenlightened head. Let us notice in passing the Christ of Puget, the original of which is at Marseilles ; here the artist errs on the side of conventionality and senti-mentalism, characteristic faults of the seventeenth century.

We must give a special place apart to a sculptured head of Christ dating from the fifteenth century which is in the collections of the Louvre (fig. 26). This head has since be-come classic, and may be found reproduced with hardly any modifi-cation in the crucifixes which have since been made. How strong is the influence of a fashion will be realized when we find in a different country, and at a much later date, that Guido Reni has taken this very head as his type and model, and reproduced it, though with some loss of power. It became in fact an artistic type, and as such was uni-versally adopted. The head is ex-pressive of the bitter moment in our Saviour's agony when He cries to His Father, " My God, My God, why hast Thou forsaken Me ? "

HEAD OF CHRIST.
LOUVRE MUSEUM (XV. CENTURY).
Fig. 26.

It is not difficult to show that we cannot look to the Flemish school of Art to give us the ideal Christ—pitiful, loving, heroic. The Christ of

Van Eyck is sufficiently well known ; it is a painting doubtless executed by that great artist about the year 1438, and is preserved to-day in the Gallery at Berlin. Nothing could be colder than this inexpressive Flemish countenance, with its enormous forehead and symmetrically arched eye-

CHRIST BLESSING.
BY QUENTIN MATSYS, ANTWERP MUSEUM (XVI. CENTURY).
Fig. 27.

brows, rising above a pair of small piercing eyes. It is the head of a man who does not think, and from whose lips we have nothing to learn.

Roger van der Veyden, a pupil of Van Eyck, is more touched by his subject. At the National Gallery there is a *Christ Crowned with Thorns* by him, which is in many ways admirable. The eyes are full of tears ; the face is full of grief and pain, the lips are slightly open. He pardons his tormentors, but all grandeur is absent from the tragedy. The sufferer is feeble, the head too long, the eyes too small. Such a Christ as this is no voluntary sacrifice—He is suffering a martyrdom from which there is no escape ; He is a mere dreamer, a victim. In another work, the triptych of the *Seven Sacraments*, the artist has depicted a yet more miserable sufferer. This is at the Antwerp Gallery. It is a *Christ upon the Cross*.

Let us now turn to Quentin Matsys, that great master of the sixteenth century. We do not much care for his *Christ, the Saviour of the World*, at the National Gallery, which, gives the figure of Christ hard and wooden, beside an exquisite Virgin. Still less do we like *The Holy Face* at Antwerp, which is a grimacing head, without light and shadow, and with a mouth singularly contorted.

But, on the other hand, attention may well be arrested by two heads, which Matsys himself may have loved to place side by side as his own conception of the Divine model, one dead, the other living. The *Christ in the Act of Blessing* of the Antwerp Museum (fig. 27) may almost be said to radiate light, but in spite of the wonderful effect which the artist has produced there is a lack of power ; we look in vain for any trace of the sacrifice which marked the life of Christ throughout. But now let us turn to the central piece of the great Antwerp triptych, *The Dead Christ* (fig. 28). Here the artist's power amounts to genius. This is in truth one of the gems of Flemish Art ; but when we analyse this great work—the Christ is in very truth dead, dead without hope of resurrection—hope, as well as life, has gone out of the corpse. Thus one of the greatest artists in two of his best paintings has not been able quite to attain the ideal. The glorious living Christ is without pity ; the dead Christ is

THE DEAD CHRIST. FRAGMENT FROM
THE ANTWERP TRIPTYCH.
BY QUENTIN MATSYS (XVI. CENTURY).
Fig. 28.

without that hidden force which has changed the whole world.

We need not allude to the works of Flemish artists of the second rank, nor to the German masters of the fifteenth century, such as Roger van der Veyden, or Bouts (whose *Christ on the Cross* is in the Berlin Gallery) ; none of these in truth rise above mediocrity. In the works of Rubens and Van Dyck we find incomparable ability, but none of that humble religious faith and feeling which is often displayed by lesser artists. We must perforce pay homage to the incomparable *Christ at Emmaus* by Rembrandt. Yes, here at last we have the true Christ of infinite goodness, love, and pitifulness, bearing on His countenance the unmistakable traces of His agony, yet emanating Divine mysterious light. In spite of these transcendent attributes, we return with satisfaction to the Christ of the Holy Shroud. Here the sacred image is instinct with greater majesty, but is imbued with so supernatural, so wonderful a calm, that as we gaze we think of His own words, " Peace I leave with you, My peace I give unto you, not as the world gives give I unto you," and the longings of the soul are appeased.

It is with some hesitation that we venture into the maze of the Italian schools in the fifteenth and sixteenth centuries ; but here as elsewhere fine examples of the conception of Christ are rare. It would be easy to show that such artists as Verrocchio, Piero della Francesca, Mantegna, and many others have very insufficiently rendered the type of Christ. Of Ghirlandajo there is in the Berlin collection a *Pieta*, where a slender-bodied Christ is supported uneasily on the knees of His mother, but the picture leaves us cold and dissatisfied.

There is no coldness about the *Christ of the Column* by Sodoma, the celebrated fresco at Sienna ; the figure might be that of a defeated gladiator, and is so pagan in feeling that we find ourselves almost regretting the miserable Christs of the Flemish school in the fifteenth century.

There is a *Dead Christ* by the Venetian master, Giovanni Bellini (fig. 29) which we may mention. The picture represents the Saviour supported by His Mother, while Saint John appears to be appealing to the spectators of this sad scene. We reproduce here a portion of the work, showing the anxious grief of the Mother, who gazes with anguish on her Son's face, in the hope of finding some last ray of hope. The Christ here is entirely human ; it is a man exhausted by the inutility of sacrifice, who has laid down his life and has definitely done with it.

Let us notice here the persistence, we might almost say the tyranny, of an art formula or tradition, which could impose itself on three such different painters as Perugino, Fra Bartolommeo, and Andrea del Sarto. The dead Christ is seen in profile; the Virgin or St. John sustains the body, while a number of spectators are grouped around in different attitudes. It is the stereotyped Italian method of treating the same scene which has been expressed by Quentin Matsys with so much force and feeling. There is no spontaneity in any one of the three painters we have mentioned; their rendering of Christ is in all equally smooth and conventional. The Christ of Andrea del Sarto, indeed, is neither more nor less than a poor repre-

THE DEAD CHRIST. BY GIOVANNI BELLINI AT VENICE (XV. CENTURY).
Fig. 29.

sentation of some beggar-man who, having fallen exhausted by the way, is surrounded by charitable and compassionate spectators.

Can we go to the immortal Raphael for the right conception of the Redeemer? Neither in the *Last Supper* at Florence, nor in his *Trans-figuration* at the Vatican, can we admit anything Divine in the aspect and attributes of the Saviour as there represented. He is one of the personages of the picture, playing His decorative part with all due fitness, just as the Apostles and others fulfil their rôles.

THE SHROUD OF CHRIST

Of choice we end our review with the *Christ* of Leonardo da Vinci (fig. 30). Was the artist right when he protested that he was powerless to deal with such a subject ?

The rough sketch of the figure is in the Brera collection at Milan.

CHRIST AT THE LAST SUPPER.
DRAWING BY LEONARDO DA VINCI AT THE BRERA MUSEUM, MILAN (XV. CENTURY).
Fig. 30.

The finished head at St. Marie des Graces is now almost indistinguishable, while in the various copies, the copyists seem to have worked according to their own fancy. It is then to the rough sketch alone that we must look for the artist's ideal; and if the original conception was pure and noble, the drawing somewhat lacks power. At first one seems to realize that the thought which the artist wished to render was that of self-abnegation, but as we continue to gaze at it we recognize that the basis of the idea is morbid and sentimental. The artist evidently drew upon his own imagination, and so we find the eyebrows commonplace in outline, the eyes vaguely prominent, the nose too rounded, and the lips weak and commonplace. Yes, Leonardo has failed, as he feared he must.

Our examination, then, has brought us to a definite conclusion; a conclusion which we believe that art-critics and men of science cannot fail to arrive at also; namely, that among all the works of art which the world has ever known, sculpture or painting, the portrait on the Holy Shroud has never been equalled, much less surpassed. It stands quite alone. Reproducing as it does, the actual lineaments of our Lord, it seems to bring Him living before us, with all the heroism, all the goodness of the Redeemer still visible on the dead face.

CHAPTER VI

*THE IMPRESSIONS ARE ACTUAL NEGATIVES—THESE NEGATIVES CAN-
NOT BE PAINTINGS — THESE NEGATIVES CANNOT HAVE BEEN
PRODUCED BY CHEMICAL TRANSFORMATION — THE SHROUD HAS
RETAINED THE IMPRESSION OF A HUMAN BODY— THE PROCESS
NECESSARY TO PRODUCE PRINTS BY SIMPLE CONTACT — THE IM-
PRESSIONS RESULT FROM SOME ACTION WITHOUT CONTACT*

THE IMPRESSIONS ARE ACTUAL NEGATIVES

AFTER the exhibition in 1898 many people asserted that the figures
on the Holy Shroud could not be paintings, for the simple reason
that they appeared as negatives. It was said, with truth, that it would be
impossible to paint thus. This argument, however, was met by a counter
assertion that the impressions might not be negatives. The first thing then
to establish is this. Are they, or are they not, negatives ?

We propose now to examine the different opinions put forward by
hostile critics who desire to prove that these are ordinary paintings by
ordinary painters, quite unworthy of the stir made about them.

In the *Chronique des Arts et de la Curiosité*, which is a supplement to
the *Gazette des Beaux Arts* of September 8, 1900 (p. 304), M. de Mély remarks that " these photographs of the Holy Shroud might be negatives,
without the impressions on the Shroud itself being of that nature. The
Shroud," he adds, " having been photographed by electric light, transparently through its substance, the paint, even though white, being opaque,
would come out dark in the photograph, and produce a negative effect."
Here M. de Mély grants that, photographically speaking, the plates of
M. Pia are correct ; other critics maintain the contrary. We wish to
avoid useless discussion, and will not argue also whether the Shroud has
or has not got opaque layers of paint upon it, or whether, if one looked
through it against the light, it would have a negative appearance. The

question to be answered is quite simple. The allegation of M. de Mély is incorrect, because the Holy Shroud *was not* photographed in the manner suggested.

We have before us an official statement of M. le Baron Antonio Manno, President of the Executive Committee of 1898, under whose supervision the whole of the photographic operations were conducted. In this duly attested document we find that the Holy Shroud, extended in its frame above the altar, was lighted from the front by two powerful electric lamps, placed about ten yards from the relic. It would not occur to any one to doubt the good faith of this Executive Committee. We may add, however, that not even this official testimony was necessary to prove that M. de Mély's statement is a mistaken one.

When we published the first edition of this work we based it on the belief (which for us was a certainty) that M. Pia's photographs were as sincere as they were scrupulously exact. We had only to look at the negative plates in our possession to ascertain that there was no trace of touching up visible, and the peculiarities and creases on the stuff were so well given that they testified to the accuracy of the original plates. But sundry of our critics, hostile to the authenticity of the Shroud, yet finding it impossible to maintain their hostile arguments without incriminating the loyalty of the Commission of 1898, have actually proceeded to do so, without the very slightest foundation for their charges. We will therefore mention here that we ourselves have been to Turin, and have seen M. Pia's original plates, and we can testify that the marks on the Holy Shroud *are* such as our illustrations represent them.

M. Pia's original negative was taken on an Edward 50 × 60 gelatine-bromo isochromatic plate (sensitive to yellow). He used a yellow screen, and a Voigtländer lens, with a diaphragm having an aperture seven millimetres in diameter. The exposure lasted eighteen minutes, with the light evenly distributed. The lens was opposite the centre of the Shroud, which is reproduced without any distortion. The plate was developed with oxalate of iron, and fixed with hyposulphite in the ordinary way. The photograph also includes the case containing the Shroud, and part of the altar, which had been temporarily erected above the high altar of the

Cathedral. The negative is excellent in every way—very finely graduated, very transparent. It has not been intensified. All the markings are clearly visible, just as we have described them. This negative is so precious that M. Pia only used it to obtain a positive on glass, from which he in turn procured a negative. These two plates were intensified, which in no way altered the picture, the only effect being to make it easier to see the details. It is from this secondary original negative that all the subsequent prints, on paper or on glass, were obtained by direct printing, the Shroud only being reproduced.

M. Pia also took two smaller photographs. One of these was taken by electric light, with five minutes' exposure, and gives the whole altar, with the Shroud diminished to the length of 13 cm. 5 mm. The other was taken in daylight, with forty-five minutes' exposure, and gives a large portion of the choir, with the entire canopy, and in the background the Chapel where the Holy Shroud is habitually preserved. On this photograph the length of the Shroud is 5 cm. 8 mm. Both photographs were taken on isochromatic plates, without a screen, and they sufficiently establish the veracity of the first precious negative. The general appearance of the Shroud is identical, and even the details are distinguishable.

The same may be said of a negative taken by M. Félice Fino, which he lent us for a fortnight. It had not been intensified, and we took two prints from it on paper. M. Fino's plate is 21 × 27, and the length of the Shroud on it is 13 centimetres. The whole altar is shown, and part of the carpet which covered the paved floor of the choir. There are also a fireman standing beside the altar, and two kneeling figures in the foreground. Add to these the instantaneous photographs reproduced by P. Solaro in his book, the duplicate of which he has been kind enough to send us, and you have the whole photographic evidence upon which our work is based.

In 1534 the Holy Shroud was strengthened by a lining of linen. In 1694 Sebastien Valfre replaced this linen lining by a black material. Finally, on April 28, 1869, the Princess Clotilde herself changed the lining, which had become worn, and replaced it by a new one of crimson silk. Thus it would have been impossible to photograph the impressions transparently through the substance of the Shroud, even if it had been desirable to do so. This is not all. Père Sanna Solaro, in his work which appeared in 1901, reproduces on page 142 an instantaneous photograph taken by one of the visitors present at the Exhibition of 1898. This valuable photograph shows the frame of the relic placed on the altar, the altar itself, and the first three rows of spectators. In this photograph the Holy Shroud and the impressions on it present the identical appearance which they do in M. Pia's fine prints. We may affirm, then, that this instantaneous photograph was not obtained by transparency.

M. de Mély admits that the plates of 1898 are genuine and normal as far as the photographic process is concerned. The argument we now have to combat is that the photographic plate has not given us a faithful image of the object itself.

The first of these critics, M. Lajoie, founds his argument on a phrase used by M. Loth in his pamphlet of 1900 : " When a photograph is taken of any person or thing, the image obtained on the sensitive plate, which appears after development, is, in consequence of the inversion of tones and the reversion of positions, the negative of the person or thing— that is to say, the contrary of what it is naturally ; it is always and necessarily a negative impression, because there is nothing in nature which is not positive. Here, by a unique exception, the impression on the Holy Shroud has produced on the photographic plate a positive."

This passage contains an error. There are certain cases when, by over-exposure, it is possible for a plate to bear a positive impression, that is to say, the exact reproduction of the object photographed, without any reversal of values. M. Loth's contention is that it is not unlikely that such conditions were realized in 1898, and that in this way may be explained the whole of the, as he thinks, ridiculous fuss made about the impressions on the Holy Shroud.

M. Pia's plate, however, is incontestably a correct negative—the black traces of burning are white ; the pieces of white material used to patch the burns are black ; the borders of the lozenge-shaped patches are light in colour, in harmony with the tone of the cloth. If M. Lajoie had not at his disposal the original photographs of M. Pia, he had only to examine the illustrations in M. Loth's pamphlet. He would have seen all this at a glance.

We have already referred to the instantaneous photograph taken at the public Exhibition, a facsimile of which was referred to above as reproduced by P. Sanna Solaro. In an instantaneous photograph there can be no question of inversion by over-exposure. Figure 16 of Père Solaro's work confirms Plate IV. of our work ; in it the marks on the Holy Shroud are visible in negative. And yet in other respects the instantaneous photograph is positive and normal ; there is the white marble altar, and the back view of the three rows of spectators is quite natural. Inversely, figure 15, in Père Solaro's work is equivalent to our Plate V. In his figure 15 the altar is black, the dark heads of the spectators are white, and, as these spectators are nearly all of them ecclesiastics, the marks of the tonsure on their heads are shown by dark circles. But on this figure 15, which is a perfectly correct negative, the modelling of the figures on the Holy Shroud are represented as positive, exactly as they are shown on the plate taken by M. Pia.

Thus M. Lajoie's objection, although given with all semblance of scientific truth, is valueless. Its author wishes to reduce all the problems raised by the Shroud of Christ to a mere confession of photographic error. The apparent mistake, however, is not that of the photographer.

We will now examine M. Chopin's objections, contained in a letter addressed to M. Chevalier, who inserted it in his *Études Critiques*, after having first requested Professor Lippmann, Member of the " Académie des Sciences " to be good enough to verify the assertions therein. Professor Lippmann examined the photographs, and recognized that the plate was normal and that the images of the Holy Shroud were incontestably negatives.

M. Chopin's letter is divided into two parts. In the first two pages the author explains how, under certain conditions, different from those indicated by M. Lajoie, plates may give direct positives ; for example, the following process will give this result : " After an ordinary light development wash the plate, cover it with a silver solution having an alkaline reaction, or any weak alkaline solution, and recommence to develop." Naturally there can be no question of M. Pia having exercised any such manipulation; but M. Chopin explains that the phenomenon may happen accidentally, and had indeed occurred to himself " in the preparation of special negatives for the reproduction of Limoges enamels." M. Chopin has then the right to use the following phrase : " There is reason to think that when this phenomenon is accidentally produced, one should seek for the cause either in a want of acidity in the silver solution or in the insufficent alkalinity of the water used for washing the plates." I do not guarantee that the terms used by M. Chopin are quite exact, and that the washing of a plate in water not sufficiently alkaline would altogether alter its character, but this is what M. Chopin says. In certain conditions it is possible that a plate may become positive without having been over-exposed.

But we will not labour the point. Such exceptional conditions were not present, since M. Pia's plate is really a negative. This point we may consider certain.

We now come to a more subtle objection, which is that although a plate may be generally negative, certain parts of it may not be perfectly so, owing to the effect of colour—yellow, for instance, often comes out black. We do not quite see how this affects our consideration of the Holy Shroud. The argument is only tenable if parts of the object are many coloured, which is not the case here.

We consider then that we have established our first position, which is that *the impressions on the Holy Shroud are really and effectively shown there in negative.*

THESE NEGATIVES CANNOT BE PAINTINGS

If the impressions on the Shroud have the character of a negative, if they are shown with the real values reversed, we cannot believe that they have been painted thus. Of two alternatives one must be taken as true : either they have been executed positively, like all paintings, and have been transformed by time into the negatives which we see, or else they are not paintings at all. Before discussing these alternatives let us see if the impressions are such as to preclude altogether the hypothesis of an ordinary painting done directly in negative fashion.

Let us quote once more from M. Chopin's letter : " M. Loth asserts that the Holy Shroud is not a painting, and that no artist, however clever, could have produced such a work in negative. As for this assertion I am of a contrary opinion, for I am fully persuaded that such crude work could easily have been produced by an artist ; but to paint in this manner would be so absurd and incomprehensible that I hesitate to assert that it was so done." Now this quotation contains two propositions, both of which we must oppose. It is not absurd for a painter to reproduce a work in negative, but if he had tried to do so he would inevitably have failed ; practically, then, we agree with M. Chopin, and will refute the hypothesis of a direct negative painting, but for different reasons than those given by him.

To begin with, with regard to a presumed painter, we will grant M. Chopin much more than he asks : we will grant that a clever artist might have painted these impressions in negative, although it scarcely seems possible to do so ; the very term " negative " has only had a meaning since the discovery of photography. The men of the fourteenth century had no reason to suspect the possibility of the inversions of lights and shades which are produced by the action of light on a sensitive plate ; but was not this much knowledge indispensable before it would occur to any one to reverse on a cloth the normal position of lights and shadows ?

But what is the point at issue ? Is it a question of the painting of a portrait, or that a certain piece of linen has been the winding-sheet of Christ ? To intelligent observers all that Christ could have left on His Shroud would be the print of His limbs and the traces of His blood, and not, properly speaking, a portrait of any sort. Now an imprint which marks the raised parts more than the hollows is in itself a negative.

It may be said that I am making things too easy for the forgers of the Middle Ages, who would not have reasoned in such subtle fashion ; that the Holy Shroud would be even more worthy of veneration had the portrait of the Saviour been clearly visible to any observer.

Well, that would simplify the question, for there would then be no hesitation in admitting that the Holy Shroud had not been painted in negative. And yet we are bound in loyalty to science to continue our argument. The arrangement of the pictures alone is enough to show us that if they really are the work of a painter, this painter has endeavoured to give them the effect of being impressions. If he were ingenious enough to know that the two bodies should lie head to head he must have also known that the impressions give us an inverted mould. To ascertain this he need only have placed his blackened hand upon a white wall, or smeared his face with red ochre and then covered it with a cloth.

In either case the marks left on the linen or on the wall could only have been caused by such portions as would appear in relief if the light shone full upon them. The half-tints and shadows on the contrary would leave fainter marks, or no marks at all. This is what fraud might have tried to reproduce in a painting.

Such an attempt must have been faulty in its execution. The real question therefore is, Are the pictures such as an artist of the fourteenth century could have executed if he had tried to imitate in his painting a true impression? M. Chopin gives a decided "yes" to this question, but our own opinion is different.

Let us imagine our painter, brushes in hand, before a large piece of cloth more than five yards long. Let us think of him as taking his measurements so that in each of the simulated impressions the different parts of the body may correspond exactly. We will suppose him accustomed to the accurate measurements and proportions of casts. We will even suppose that, gifted with preternatural ingenuity, he would know how to assign to the thighs, the calves, the ankles, the extraordinary forms visible on the Shroud, the whole thing done in order to deceive pilgrims who in truth would have been satisfied with less exactitude. We will even suppose him clever enough to avoid all the pit-falls which nature prepares for us when we try to counterfeit her by art.

It is in the modelling of the face that we shall detect our painter.

With a simple object it is easy enough to invert the lights and shades, to reproduce the aspect of an ordinary geometrical figure, such as a cube, a cylinder, or a sphere in negative. But examine Plate II.; search therein for any markings which could have served to facilitate the execution of a fraud.

Whatever M. Chopin may say, nothing could be less regular, nothing could be more unexpected than the nose, the eyebrows, cheek-bones and cheeks ; nothing more obscure than the forehead and the hair and the modelling of the mouth. On Plate II., beneath the nose, a succession of tints are strangely blended, dark and light alternatively. No one could even interpret them without the aid of Plate III. How could these markings have been invented which are so hard to read on the holy Shroud ? Of course, *after* closely examining the facsimile of the negative on Plate III., which gives their real signification to all the features, we can go back to our examination of the linen cloth and interpret it rightly ; but will any one tell us by what process a negative model could have been executed so that the author, whilst at work upon it, could have judged of what its effect would be when inverted and brought back to its positive condition.

But we go too far. The hypothesis is absurd, and could not be maintained unless the Holy Shroud, instead of being what it is, resembled the copies which have been made of it, such as the Shroud of Besançon.

We must not take a step forward without investigating all the objections which might by any possibility arise.

Could a fraudulent artist of the Middle Ages by any known artifice have executed a head in negative on the linen cloth ? A negative does not exist in nature, but in certain conditions a negative may be simulated. Place your hand flat against a window ; the fingers, with the light shining just behind them, appear as they would in a negative. The same with the cheeks and nose, if looked at in the same way.

But shut your hand and look towards the light through your closed fist. No matter how bright the light, the crevices between the fingers will remain dark ; yet in a real negative these crevices would be light ! In a head we have not only to reckon with prominent features, such as the nose and cheeks ; there are also the eyes and mouth to be considered, and no amount of light would change their normal aspect.

Further argument seems unnecessary.

Here is another hypothesis—so ingenious that it arouses our admiration.

Suppose we take a large blackboard and draw a figure on it in brown chalk. The chalk will stand out light against the black background ; therefore we can mass it thickly for the high lights, and let the black show through the chalk for the deepest shadows. The portrait finished, transfer it on to a white cloth by laying the cloth on the blackboard. Behold we have a negative.

The thickest part of the chalk will now be the deepest shadow, and *vice versâ*, just as in the Shroud. But the difficulty will be to give the modelled contours. We cannot *outline* our figure in chalk, because on our blackboard the chalk represented the high lights. This knowledge of technique is just possible in a frequenter of the studios of to-day ; but such a complicated process as we have described would have been impossible for the painters of the Middle Ages.

Here then is another step gained. We proved that the impressions on the Shroud are negatives ; *now we know that such negatives could not have been produced by any pictorial process.*

THESE NEGATIVES CANNOT HAVE BEEN PRODUCED BY CHEMICAL TRANSFORMATION

If it is claimed that the stains on the Shroud are the work of some painter, then we must assume that they were painted in the positive or ordinary manner ; further, we must admit that the chemical change wrought by the centuries which have elapsed since their imprint has transformed this positive painting into the negative which we have to-day. If this hypothesis is not tenable we must give up the idea that the Holy Shroud has been painted.

It is M. Chopin again who puts forward this new hypothesis.

He maintains that the picture on the Shroud, though not a real negative—i.e. a negative to our human eye—is nevertheless a photographic negative. He admits that the light colours, without undergoing visible inversion, may none the less have become impervious to photography, and thus even more inert than the shadows. He even suggests that the dark tones may in part have disappeared.

Our answer is that the human eye could perfectly well distinguish a negative picture on the Shroud.

The technical arguments used by M. Chopin to explain this possible change in the quality of the colours as regards photographic effect may be used with equal reason to support the hypothesis of some change which has taken place and is perceptible to the human eye.

We will quote M. Chopin's own words :

" The flesh tints *may* have been painted with a mixture of white paint, which is usually an oxide of lead or of zinc combined with reds (sulphate of mercury), ochres, or naturally tinted earths ; the shadows *may* have been done with black paint mixed with the same ochres and natural or burnt earths, or even with bitumen. The lighter portions painted thickly and the shadows less so, in order to give depth.

" Painted in this way, which is the ordinary way, the Holy Shroud passed through critical periods, such as the fire at the Sainte Chapelle in 1532, when the constitution of its colours must have been considerably modified. The oxides of lead in the light colours must have become clouded by the sulphur of mercury in the reds, or by external causes, such as one always sees at work in old paintings. The natural earths may have been calcined by the heat—the bitumen burnt, evaporated, vanished !— all this is possible.

" What would now remain after the fire ? A rude image whereon all the light tints which had been mixed with white would be proportionately black, and portions of which would be more or less obliterated."

We can dispose at once of the theory regarding the fire of 1532, since, as we have shown in Chapter IV., the impressions were already negatives at the end of the fourteenth century.

We must also call M. Chopin's attention to the fact that painting executed in zinc medium does not get blackened by sulphur ; this, however, is of little consequence, painting with a lead medium being much more usual.

Again, it is not the case that the early painters painted in high lights very thickly, and it is not a good method to give depth to the shadows by painting thinly. To-day we know many painters do this, but always at the expense of the *clairoscuro*.

It is unnecessary to make too much of these trifling points. M. Chopin passes in review the causes which may produce alteration in old paintings.

The fresco as it is actually seen.

The fresco as seen on the negative plate.

CALVARY

Fragment of a fresco at Assisi.

Such alterations are generally produced by the action of sulphur on colours whose main ingredient is lead.

It is more difficult to see how the shadows could get darker in proportion to the light parts getting lighter, but this must be the case if our opponent is to prove his case.

We will ourselves cite an example far more convincing than any cited by M. Chopin in support of his own theory.

In the upper church at Assisi there are a series of frescoes hitherto attributed to Cimabuë. Tourists as a rule pay little attention to these paintings, which are much dilapidated and extremely ugly ; but last year a friend of mine, knowing of the experiments undertaken at the " Sorbonne " in connexion with the Holy Shroud, was struck by the fact that in the frescoes representing the Crucifixion a whole group of figures appeared to be painted negatively. My friend called my attention to this remarkable fact, and I at once procured a photograph of the fresco. An enlarged fragment of this photograph is reproduced on Plate VI.

The upper part of the plate shows the painting in its actual condition. The sky remains light, and the aureole of the figure on the left is still represented in a normal manner ; but the heads and draperies are absolutely negative. The transposition is not complete throughout the fresco, and the figures below a sharply defined limit remain positive. The limit corresponds to a change in the plaster on which they are painted. Under the facsimile of the fresco we have placed the reproduction of the photographic plate, giving the portions whith were negative in the fresco restored to their positive condition, whilst the sky and the figures on the left are now negative. The plate has been reproduced, so as to give this aspect of the fresco, and also in order that the reader may easily recognize the figures and may get the impression of the work as the painter intended it to be.

This inversion of the picture, the result of chemical change, is particularly striking in the head which occupies the centre of the picture. Before its inversion this head was a really remarkable portrait, but the flesh-tints have now become almost black and the beard completely white. M. Chopin could hardly desire to find a seemingly better example in favour of his thesis. The chemical change produced in so regular a manner hardly alters the artistic value of the painting, and many of the heads are very beautiful.

Granted that it is possible for a painting such as the fresco at Assisi, or a Byzantine icon, to become absolutely negative under certain exceptional conditions, we still contend that it is impossible for the figures on the Holy Shroud to be affected in the same way. For this we give three distinct reasons, the importance of which will be at once recognized.

In the first place, the very fact that the material of the Shroud is very light and supple proves that it could not carry the amount of paint requisite for a picture which could change in the manner described. If such a painting had ever been made on this cloth it would have long since crumbled away and have left hardly any trace.

Let us consider the question of a painting either in oil or water-colour, these being the only methods which need be considered when chemical inversions are in question. Oil-colours with a lead base, whether mixed with sulphide of mercury or not, constitute insoluble substances ; they can only be moistened with oil or water. They then form a semi-fluid paste, and can be spread over the required surface in layers, which may vary in thickness.

When water is used to moisten such paint, a little gum or albumen is added to give the required elasticity and to make it adhere to the canvas. That done, the painting may be preserved as long as the cloth remains flat. Even to roll it up would be unwise, unless it were rolled over a cylinder of fairly large diameter. It would be quite impossible to fold it like a hand-kerchief, as the painting would crumble off at the folds almost at once. Also, so long as the picture remained on it, the cloth would lose all its flexi-bility, for the threads would be clogged together by the paint.

Consider any oil-painting. Oil-paint adheres much more firmly than water-colour, and does not flake off so easily. We all know how rigid a canvas becomes when covered with oil-paint. Even before beginning to paint with colour, a coat of white lead is commonly spread over the canvas, sufficient to make it quite stiff.

These facts are well known. Every one has handled or seen canvases prepared for oil painting. Painting with gum is less well known, being now very little used for large pictures. It is used sometimes for screens made of light gauze, and if the painting is taken out of its frame and rubbed between the fingers the paint quickly scales off in powder and is effaced.

Many ancient paintings in water-colour are well known. Only last year a number of persons met at the Guimet Museum to see the curios found by M. Gazet in the Greco-Egyptian tombs of Upper Egypt. I particularly recall the full-length portrait of a certain Thaïs. The regular features of the painted face, the black eyes elongated by henna. The elegance of her ornaments contrasted strangely with the miserable remains of her mummy, placed close by. One Serapion, with his body bound round with heavy iron rings, was a still more lugubrious figure. The painted cloth was almost completely rigid, and the paint had worn off at the creases. Paint, and paint alone, had made the cloth stiff ; without the paint it would have been an ordinary limp wrapping-cloth.

The Holy Shroud is a very supple cloth, like our modern linen. Since it is still perfectly flexible in all its parts, and since the figures on it have not disappeared, we may affirm that there is on it no painting executed in any of the above media.

If questioned as to how we are able to assert that the Holy Shroud is supple (apart from the testimony of those who handled it), we refer again to the photographs of M. Pia.

We have only to look at these photographs to see that the cloth, although backed and strengthened with silk, has remained slightly creased. The inequalities formed by the creases have made many slight differences in the tones of the photograph, showing that the material is very supple and is kept stretched with difficulty. One of these creases cuts the head a little above the forehead ; another just below the chin. There are many others, which will at once be noticed. They appear as black lines in Plate iv., because they throw a shadow on the Shroud, and inversely they are white in Plate v. The fineness of the lines shows the thinness of the material.

But we may learn more than this from these photographs.

The Holy Shroud is now kept rolled up in a casket ; folds are avoided as far as possible, the cloth being so old and easily worn in the creases.

But formerly no such precautions were taken. The burnt places and water-stains show how the cloth was folded at the time of the fire in 1532—just as any ordinary cloth might be folded, lengthways, right down the middle. This crease passed almost down the centre of the face. Had any paint been on the Holy Shroud, the form of the face must have been completely destroyed.

What we have already said should satisfy the most exacting critic. Nevertheless we wished to make other experiments on cloths similar to that of the Holy Shroud, experiments suggested by our examination of the photographs.

For this purpose we consulted M. Gazet, the distinguished author of *Les Fouilles du Faijum*, and M. Terme, the learned Director of the textile museum at Lyons. These gentlemen were extremely interested by the photographs of the Holy Shroud, and placed at our disposal a series of ancient Egyptian cloths collected in the tombs of Faijum. With these cloths we have established a scale of thickness, so that we have been able to ascertain which materials when stretched bore the closest resemblance to the Holy Shroud as represented in the photographs. We have thus determined a sort of standard which should very nearly represent the quality of the Shroud at Turin.

This material is so fine that it is almost linen muslin.

Satisfied on this point, we had a water-colour painting made on very soft and fine material, mixing white lead with the gum. Such a medium only adheres to the material when it is applied in the form of a very thin wash with a very small quantity of white lead. But no representation of a body could be obtained with so liquid a mixture. It was necessary to paint over this first wash in light and dark tones. A picture was thus obtained, very thin in substance but very fragile. The paint came off at the least touch as soon as the cloth was folded.

This is not all. There are doubtless to-day very few people who have been permitted to hold the Holy Shroud in their hands. We have been fortunate enough to secure the testimony of one of these privileged persons, who accompanied Princess Clotilde when it was shown to the public in 1868. This precious witness, who really handled the Shroud, certified

NOT PRODUCED BY CHEMICAL TRANSFORMATION

that the cloth was unusually and strikingly supple. We have now a perfect right to conclude that the impressions cannot be pictures executed in water-colour or in oils.

If therefore they are the handiwork of a painter, they must be executed in wash, with a medium of turpentine, or, better still, a dye. In this case the high lights would either have been left untouched or indicated with a light glaze. But such a painting could not possibly have become a negative by any combination of sulphur, as a painting with body-colour mostly composed of white lead might have done.

We argue thus to prove that the figures are not formed by a chemical inversion of colours.

The Holy Shroud is *not* a painting which has formed a negative by the action of sulphur in the light tints. Such a picture would be one on which the light tints had gone very black. Whatever might have been their original tones, such colours take on the livid tint which sulphur of lead communicates to the substances with which it is mixed.

The entire figures on the Holy Shroud are formed in reddish-brown tints. Had they been painted they would have faded, not become darker.

We are fully justified in this assertion by the descriptions given in past ages, and by careful examination of the copies of the Holy Shroud; we can also rely on the testimony of several distinguished inhabitants of Chambéry, who were able in 1898 to make a leisurely examination of the Holy Shroud.

We know that in 1898 the Holy Shroud was visible for eight days, from May 25 to June 2. M. de Buffet, a learned inhabitant of Chambéry, gave us a circumstantial description of the Shroud and the impressions on it. So did Dom Lafond, a learned Benedictine monk, and others, whom we need not mention. The figures, seen close, look like a series of brownish stains, which get fainter at the edges and merge gradually into the light background of the cloth, but seen from further off stand out clearly. Dom Lafond assured us that at a distance of twenty-five yards, he saw them better even than on the photograph. In the sacristy adjoining the Sainte Chapelle at Turin there is a water-colour copy, life size, done in 1898. To

123

have reproduced all the details would have involved much work, but the general effect is faithful.

M. Manus and M. Pia, who examined bits of the linen on which we tried our chemical experiments described in our final chapter (producing pictures by the action of ammoniacal vapour on linen impregnated with oil and aloes), were struck with the wonderful resemblance between my pictures so obtained and the impressions on the Holy Shroud.

Just lately we have tried another experiment. Allowing water to soak into parts of our linen impressions, we have thus obtained dark markings identical with those on the Shroud caused by the water used to extinguish the fire of 1532.

Recent critics cite testimony to prove that the impressions in the Middle Ages were much more strongly marked then than they are now, but there is no means of coming to a conclusion on this point. Certainly photography reveals details with extraordinary minuteness which have been entirely lacking in even the most faithful copies of the Middle Ages, and we think ourselves justified in saying that the Shroud has not essentially changed since it has been known historically.

Our most obstinate opponents bring forward quite different arguments to the two we have cited; they admit freely that the figures are not paintings changed into negatives — in fact I think that all careful observers must see at a glance that the Shroud could not have been painted by an artist.

All sorts of marks are distinguished in the photographs, which tend to prove that the Holy Shroud retains the impression of a body.

We have already alluded briefly to these marks in the first chapter; we will now return to them in the detail to which the subject is entitled. These markings are particularly important from the moment that the observer renounces the hypothesis that the figures have been fraudulently obtained by painting a direct negative, and begins to think that the negatives are the result of chemical action.

In order to paint this negative directly on the Holy Shroud the ingenious artist must have known the work required of him, and must have been able to imitate the conditions of a natural impression. But in the hypothesis which we are now discussing the author of these impressions could only have been a simple painter, and could only have executed an ordinary portrait on the cloth. We can no longer therefore consider the marks as the perverted ingenuity of a forger, for, artistically speaking, they could have no meaning.

Thus, as we analyze the hypothesis on which our opponents rely, in attributing the execution of the pictures on the Holy Shroud to some artist of the Middle Ages, we perceive that such arguments are untenable.

It would have been easier to have stated these arguments in a few lines and to have left our readers to examine for themselves the traces visible on the Shroud at Turin. Any unprejudiced observer must arrive at the same conclusion as ourselves.

But objections have been made ; and some persons, who have not even seen the photographs, or who have glanced carelessly at the plates, profess themselves convinced by the criticisms of MM. Chopin, Lajoie, or de Mély. Thus M. de Mély has just published a pamphlet entitled *Le Saint Suaire de Turin est-il Authentique (Pussielgue)*, which contains many observations which are quite inexact, and which we can easily refute.

The Holy Shroud is in itself a very remarkable—we may even say unique—object, if we consider the exceptional circumstances which must have produced the impressions, even without reference to their true signification. It is well therefore to say clearly what they *are not*. This negative statement will prepare the way for the positive study which we now propose to undertake. We will once more mark the limit of what we consider proved by the foregoing arguments. Since the impression is neither a painting executed in negative, nor an ordinary painting transformed by chemical action, then it must be recognized that *the figures on the Holy Shroud are in no sense the work of man.*

THE SHROUD HAS RETAINED THE IMPRESSION OF A HUMAN BODY

If the figures on the Holy Shroud are not the work of man, they must be what they seem to be ; that is to say—impressions. A body—we do not yet say a corpse—has really been laid on this cloth in the manner indicated by the figures. This is a great step gained. All our efforts so far have been to dispel misunderstanding. Now we approach the problem itself.

The Holy Shroud, then, has retained the print of a human body. Does this mean that all idea of fraud is now at an end. By no means. It is possible to assert that the forger at Lirey, though not a painter, had some common sense. In his efforts to represent a cloth as the Shroud of Christ he may very well have reasoned as follows :

" Let us cover a human body with some colouring matter and envelope it in a large sheet ; we shall obtain the imprint of the body, after which it will be easy to persuade people that the body was that of Christ."

We will now inquire how the forger would set to work, and what results he would be likely to obtain. This investigation should prove that it was beyond his power to make the impressions visible on the actual Shroud. But before ourselves undertaking this new investigation we will put forward the reflections made by M. Chevalier on this point in a pamphlet which appeared in 1902.

We were somewhat surprised to read on page 13 in this work by M. Chevalier the following sentence : " Nevertheless it is not enough to eliminate the possibility of a negative being painted—it must be established how the negative became fixed on the sheet."

Surely it is for the supporters, not the opponents, of the fraud hypothesis to establish how the work was done. We shall feel we have gained a point if we are able to refute all the theories which attribute the work to a forger.

To find satisfaction in the lines quoted above we should have to admit that M. Chevalier had a whole arsenal of suppositions at his disposal. He might say, " Although these figures are not the work of a painter, they may be the result of some mechanical process."

But M. Chevalier does not suggest any new explanation. On the contrary, on page 39 we find him warmly criticizing the hypothesis of mechanical process brought forward by Father Sanna Solaro. This writer believes in the authenticity of the Shroud, but he also believes that the impressions thereon are the result of direct contact.

IMPRESSION OF HUMAN BODY RETAINED

M. Chevalier does not accept this theory, and we quote his brief and energetic refutation :

" The author supposes that the bleeding body would have left a print at all points where it was in contact with the cloth (p. 122 of P. Solaro). There are many ways of proving the impossibility of this explanation. I am astonished that a sometime professor of physical science can suggest the possibility of such a phenomenon ; an impression is one thing—a portrait, even a negative portrait, quite another. He had only to try the experiment on a willing subject."

" This has been done by an Italian doctor, Dr. P. Caviglia. Le P. S. S. (le Père Solaro) may see the results in the journal *Presente et Avenire* (Roma, re ann., p. 139). They are contemptible ; yet in this way they claim to have demonstrated the authenticity of the Shroud of Turin ! The final argument is worthy of those which preceded it."

P. Sanno Solaro's adversary has not spared him.

But in what a position has M. Chevalier placed himself ? On page 13 he admits that we may put aside all idea of fraud by a painter. On page 39 he disposes of the idea of a fraudulent manipulator. We are obliged to return to our first theory. Surely M. Chevalier must hold in reserve, in order to attribute it to the forger, some extraordinary method which owes nothing to the skill of artists and which can make a negative by other means than contact. He certainly must mean to tell us that the man in 1353 already knew the secrets of photography.

M. Chevalier declares himself not convinced when we demonstrate that the figures on the Shroud are not paintings, yet he refuses to admit that they are prints by contact.

It remains for him to suggest new arguments.

In a scientific work we have not the right to put aside the possibility of impression by contact as lightly as M. Chevalier does.

If the prints obtained by Dr. Caviglia are as formless as M. Chevalier represents, it may be because the subject was covered with coloured grease and not with powder.

All greasy substances, all aromatic mixtures, would only produce blotches of about the same tint. The colouring substance might be of irregular thickness, and might get blotted ; but it would not shade off in the way necessary to produce a real modelling.

But there is no necessity to cover the subject with grease ; red chalk would give a less coarse result. A ferruginous earth, such as burnt Sienna or red ochre, reduced to impalpable powder, will adhere fairly well to a cloth such as we have in question. To make this adherence reliable—that is to say, to fix the drawing—it will be sufficient to spray the cloth with a liquid albumen, or more simply to drench it with very liquid gum. What amount of sensitiveness would there be in such a method of getting an impression ? Hardly any, you may say ; but this is not quite the case.

We may reason thus. The portions of the body which touch the cloth would stain it in a uniform manner, and those which did not touch the cloth would make no mark. Consequently the impression would not be modelled. This is not all. To reproduce the rounded portions it would be necessary to touch them. Therefore, when the print was completed and the cloth which had been on the receding portions was laid out flat, the figure would be considerably enlarged.

This is why we cannot hope to obtain by simple contact good reproductions of a delicate object, such as the human face. It is possible, however, for a careful operator to place the linen in such a way as to obtain perfect shaded modelling, and it should not be impossible to go further and obtain satisfactory results.

In this way the sculptor and modellist, M. le Dr. P. Recher, so well known for his works in artistic anatomy, wished to show me the tracings he had obtained by making patients suffering from *locomotor attaxi* walk on long slips of paper after smearing their feet with red chalk. The patient, walking with his ordinary tread, himself diagnoses his illness.

For Dr. Recher's purpose it matters very little whether the prints of the feet are well modelled or not, but as a matter of fact these impressions are really good.

The foot in its different parts presses very unequally on the paper. There is every shade of difference between the energetic pressure made by the heel and the ball of the foot and the delicate contact of the instep.

PRINTS PRODUCED BY SIMPLE CONTACT

The outer side of the sole of the foot presses almost as strongly as the heel ; but working inward from this outer edge a point is soon reached at which all contact is lost and the impression ceases.

The impression is not lost quite as soon as might be imagined, as the instep bends somewhat under the weight of the body and the toes and heels sink in a remarkable manner. Also the paper which is compressed in the places where the pressure is greatest rises itself under the arch of the instep.

The fact which we find interesting is that the red lead adheres to the paper better and more thickly where the pressure has been strongest, and further that the impression thus given is in negative, because the round parts, which make the strongest impression, would be in highest relief if the sole of the foot were looked at in the light and yet represented by the darkest tones. In the impressions obtained by Dr. Recher there are no deformations, as the foot can be applied directly on a flat surface.

THE PROCESS NECESSARY TO PRODUCE PRINTS BY SIMPLE CONTACT

To make the experiment choose an object which can readily be represented on a flat surface—do not try to obtain great depth of effect—try to reproduce the modellings in their relative values by pressing gently with the hand over the subject which the linen covers.

And we may here allude to a want of similarity in Dr. Recher's prints by direct contact, namely that the inside modelling of the foot is shaded, but that the contours have a hard outline ; and this is natural. The patient in walking plants his heel firmly ; after resting a moment on his toes, he loses contact with the paper as he walks along, and the impression suddenly ends. The shading corresponding to the distance between the object smeared with red lead and the cloth which receives the impression *should* be the same on the outside of the print as it is on the inside. It should be so if an impression is to be complete, and it is so in the Holy Shroud.

This criticism is not of a very serious nature, and if the theory of a forger making false impressions by some mechanical process could be met in no better way we would at once admit that with a little additional skill it might have been done. The means are simple. If the shading of the contours is desired, rub gently with the finger when the print is finished in such a way as to graduate them, and it is done.

But some shading may be done without intention. Let us suppose that we are going to take the print of the front view of a corpse lying on the ground. We should firmly press the cloth along the central line of the body and more lightly on the sloping surfaces, graduating our passes so that the general contours take form by degrees.

We specify the front view because it would not be the same if the print were made by a figure lying *on* a piece of cloth. In that case every point where the body had pressed heavily would seem flat and hard at the edges, just as did the footprint. To round off the outlines it would be necessary to rub them with the finger.

This demonstration is not without value, because it shows us that it is possible to produce the imprint of a corpse on a cloth like that of Turin fraudulently as far as the trunk and limbs were concerned, but utterly impossible to so produce an impression of the head, as we shall see.

In the foregoing arguments we have pleaded the cause of the forger, and have made concessions in his favour which even M. Chevalier seems indisposed to grant. These concessions were legitimate and necessary, but we cannot concede more ; and we now affirm that it is impossible by simple contact, even with after corrections, to reproduce a human head.

We will suppose the forger to be at his work, trying to obtain such an impression as may be seen on the Holy Shroud.

Our first remark is that the sides of the face starting from the cheek-bones have not touched the cloth (we have already mentioned the small lateral cushions used in mummy burial). Secondly, we see at the sides two locks of hair which seem to have been stiffened and thickened. This hair is on a level with the cheek-bones. As the body is lying on its back, these locks of hair, if they had been free, would by their natural weight have fallen back on the general mass of hair which the back impression reproduces very well. These two strands of hair then must have been separated from the rest, and when the head was bowed forward may have become coagulated with dust and sweat, though this would scarcely suffice to produce this effect. Or these two locks of hair may have rested on the lateral cushions.

We have a second reason for suggesting that there were cushions or similar supports placed on each side of the head. In the front impression the shoulders do not appear, therefore the cloth did not touch this part of the body ; it must have been supported on each side of the head and must have rested again on the chest lower down.

Supposing the forger to have realized all this, he would not have committed the mistake of letting the cloth envelop the nose, nor would he have allowed it to press against the sunken portions of the face as closely as the raised parts.

We will credit him with all the skill that he might have acquired in making prints similar to those of Dr. Recher. The operator, we will say, has stretched the linen with great care, fixing the edges ; he will be content to let the cloth rest on the bridge of the nose, on the forehead, and on the chin ; also on the cheek-bones. To make the modelling possible he will have made the cloth touch the sloping portions, such as the sides of the nose, lightly. He will have endeavoured to let it touch the lips with great delicacy.

Under these conditions even the eyeballs might give an impression which need not be too pronounced.

We have ourselves submitted personally to such an experiment at the Sorbonne, and are therefore able to describe from experience the method which the forger of Lirey might have employed if he had had the patience and skill.

The writer lay down on an operating-table, and his face was carefully smeared with red chalk. The same thing had been done to a false beard which was fixed on to his face in order to approach as nearly as possible to the conditions indicated on the print ; in order also to bring all the lower part of the face to one plane. Dr. E. Herouard, Maître de Conférences at the Sorbonne, and his friend and colleague, M. Robert, Associate of the University, proceeded personally to try and take a print. They were well acquainted with the impressions on the Holy Shroud, and wished to assure themselves as to the possibility of such a portrait being produced by simple contact.

THE SHROUD OF CHRIST

On Plate VII. we reproduce the three best of these impressions. The three upper heads are the facsimiles of the proofs reduced in size. Below each is its negative print. The cloths bearing the impressions were the equivalents of the Holy Shroud ; the negatives are equivalent to those of M. Pia given on our Plates III. and V.

It will be seen that we radically failed in our attempt to reproduce by a mechanical process impressions similar to those on the Shroud. The best of our attempts is the centre one, and it is very poor.

The print on the left has the nose abnormally developed—the head on the linen is that of a negro ; on the negative it resembles that of a drowned man. The head on the right had the cloth as lightly strained as possible, but the more the cloth was strained over the bridge of the nose the more it made it appear like a hard right angle without modelling and without any sign of the sides of the nose on the cloth ; in their place there is a complete gap, white on the cloth, black on the negative.

The great fault in all three heads is that the eyes are lowered almost to the line of the nostrils, and the cheek-bones and mouth are also in their wrong places, and the cheeks seem swollen. In all the specimens which we reproduce there is some change in the general proportions of the face. In vain the operator tries to alter or correct. It would be impossible to consider the rough print as a sketch, only needing to be touched up to gain the requisite expression. Artists know that a likeness exists in the very first, slightest sketch. If the sketch starts badly, better destroy it at once—to work on a bad beginning where the harmonies are false is to lose one's power of judgment ; unconsciously the eye tries to reconcile the model to the bad sketch, which one has not had the courage to sacrifice.

It is useless to enter into further details—to show, for instance, that the beard was not represented though thickly charged with colour and supported from underneath in order to secure its contact with the linen. It was impossible to establish any parallel between our efforts and the impressions on the Shroud. We obtained a face after a fashion, but the features are so distorted that it is only a caricature.

One thing seems certain, if the forger at the Abbey of Lirey had been reduced to work in the way we did, he would never have obtained a portrait

Photographic facsimiles of three impressions.

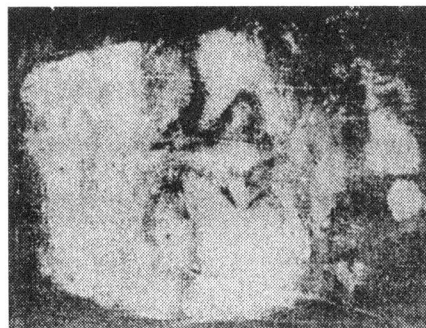

which could stand photography. On the Shroud, if the features are faint in places, the proportions remain admirable ; and the powerful effect they produce is mainly due to the perfect harmony which they present as a whole.

The forger could doubtless have obtained the imprints of a body and limbs by simple contact, but he could *not* have obtained the portrait of a head ; this theory must be abandoned.

No one could assert that the head and the body have been obtained by different processes ; in fact, on the Shroud the entire figures are in harmony with the same geometrical laws, and present the same general characteristics.

At the same time, if the forger had obtained a head no better than those in our illustration he would probably have been quite content with that result, bad as it is. His work would not have been criticized so long as no photographic camera led to an investigation of it.

In conclusion, even if the forger had wished to do better than our effort at the Sorbonne, he could have had no means by which to realize his good intention. In short, no worker by any known pictorial method could have executed the figures on the Holy Shroud.

We have now ascertained two more important points.

The figures on the Holy Shroud *are* impressions.

These impressions cannot have been obtained by contact only.

But these two propositions involve a corollary of even greater importance.

It is impossible any longer to attribute the figures on the Holy Shroud to a forger.

Before registering this important conclusion we should like to run rapidly through the evidence which has led us to this result.

Have we employed the ordinary forms of reasoning ?—by induction or by deduction ? Truly we do not know, having been so much occupied in presenting our contentions in their simplest and most obvious form. The figures being negative, whence came the negatives ? Could an ordinary painter have so manipulated his medium as to produce this negative ?

Impossible.

THE SHROUD OF CHRIST

Could an ordinary and positive painting become changed into a negative by the effect of chemical transformation ?

Assuredly this has not been the case.

Is there any possible method by which a forger in the Middle Ages
could have produced the effect of a negative ?

We answer that there *is* such a method (as we have just seen) but
that the results are so imperfect that a positive and natural photographic
portrait could not be obtained from them, such as has been obtained
from the impressions on the Shroud.

Therefore we may dismiss the question of forgery.

If we have departed from fact in this long chain of argument we are
still open to conviction, but we now think ourselves justified in saying
that *the impressions shown on the Holy Shroud have been spontaneously
produced.*

THE IMPRESSIONS RESULT FROM SOME ACTION WITHOUT CONTACT

It remains for us to discover the natural law which has produced these
impressions, which are something more than stains.

We have pointed out the grave defects which there must be in all impressions *made by contact* which attempt to reproduce the natural image of
a delicately moulded subject. We shall try to learn what sort of action
other than direct contact has influenced the production of the impressions
on the Shroud of Turin.

Every painting represents things not as they are in reality, but as they
appear when projected on a flat surface. Impressions by simple contact
cannot produce this effect. Yet this is what we find on the Shroud of
Turin.

Take any solid object—a sphere, a cube—no matter what Suspend
it in the air and look at it from underneath. Draw it in this position ; the
drawing has the same form as the projection of the object on a horizontal
plane. In other words, if from a number of points on our object we let
fall the same number of weighted threads, these threads will mark out in
plan a figure which is the *projection* of the suspended object. The drawing
will be identical with this projection if it is the same size as the object

drawn. If we make the drawing smaller, it will not be the same size, but will be in strict proportion to it.

It is not easy to draw from below an object suspended overhead, but our argument holds good from whatever position we look at an object.

We will only deal as yet with objects of little depth. If our drawing has to represent numerous concave objects on different planes we shall have to consider not only the laws of projection, but also those of perspective. It is enough that every picture represents a fragment of nature reproduced upon a flat surface.

So much for the outline ; but we have yet to consider the shading by which this outline, though flat, shall be made to resemble rounded or hollowed forms.

Here we have no fixed rules. All depends on the way the light falls on the object. We must endeavour to give faithfully the relative shadows as our eyes see them. The portions which receive the rays of light directly will be more highly illumined than the parts which fall away from the light. In like manner the concave surfaces will be darker than the convex.

Let us examine the back of a hand held quite straight with the fingers close together, so that the light falls full upon it. The moulding of the fingers will be as we have described, and the hollows between the fingers will be in dark shadow, deepening where the fingers come in contact.

These facts are familiar to every one, and there is no need to enter into longer explanations of what is lacking in the case of contact-prints. The representation of the head on the Holy Shroud cannot be a print made in this way.

In Plate III. the head looks as if the concave and convex surfaces had been projected on a plane, that is to say drawn or photographed. The modelling is almost as if the light had been from the front. I say *almost* because some parts seem shaded as if the light came from above, but I shall allude to these further on. This head, then, may be said to be almost the equivalent of a drawing, or even of an ordinary photograph taken through a lens. Yet we know that it is not a drawing, and if it is something of the nature of a photograph it is certainly not an ordinary one. We are speaking now of the head converted to the positive. Let us look at it as it is actually seen on the cloth (Plates II. and IV.). Here we see it projected on a plane, but with all the modelling reversed. The convex portions are the darkest, the hollows are the lightest, just as if it were printed by contact.

But note this difference, a most important one. There is no distortion in the features, and the modelling, though it seems elementary, is yet so correct that the head, in its positive aspect, looks like a drawing by a good artist.

We are nearing the solution of our problem, or at least the partial solution, and shall shortly understand the physical characteristics of the impression on the Holy Shroud.

In the first place it really is a sort of imprint or impression, and it conforms to the general rules of impressions. On the one hand, if the cloth is stretched flat, it will rest only on prominent parts of the body ; on the other hand, if the cloth is not flat, if it is wrapped round the body, it will come in contact with the different planes of the body successively, and the impression will be thus greatly distorted.

In the case in point, if we look for the sides of the face, the shoulders, the ears, the neck, we shall not find them—*we must conclude that the linen has not touched those parts.* On the other hand, in the front view of the figure, the calves, and also the ankles, which coincide approximately with the lower edge of the photograph, bear evident traces of wrapping. Thus the impression is distorted in the one instance by too much contact, and in the other by too little.

But the figures are produced by some more delicate process than simple contact, since in many parts of the body, and notably on the face, the modelling is excellent.

In the front view of the figure there is no deformation of the parts where the linen lay in approximately one plane.

But if nevertheless in these very places there is also shaded modelling, as in a drawing, it must indicate that on this stretched linen a projection has taken place. *Some emanation from the body has acted on the linen,* and since the hollows on the Shroud are less vigorously reproduced than the raised portions it must be admitted that this *something* worked with less intensity in proportion as the distance from the body increased.

Is not the law which this *something* followed simply the *law of distance* which governs all natural phenomena ? Under this law effect increases or decreases as the square of the distance, in more or less degree, dependent upon attendant conditions.

In the present case it is indeed hard to determine with what rapidity the unknown action took place between the body and the Shroud ; the main point is that we can assert that the action diminished in proportion as the distance of the body from the Shroud increased. We may almost affirm that the decrease was rapid, as the cloth has evidently not received any impression from certain portions of the face and body, no doubt those from which it was too far distant. Thus it is that before making any detailed examination we are able to assert that the impressions are negatives, because the raised parts of the body are reproduced strongly while the hollows have given fainter impressions in proportion to their distance from the cloth.

A print by simple contact, we have seen, produces a negative impression, but a very rough and coarse negative.

In order that the body should act on the cloth, actual contact—no matter how slight—is required. The print on the Holy Shroud is a still more perfect negative, because the image has been also in part produced *without* contact. Nevertheless we do not pretend that this negative is as true a one as if it had been taken by means of a lens.

To sum up : an impression has been formed on the Shroud. The figure produced is not to be called a photograph, because light has had no part in forming it. In the language of science it is the result of *action at a distance* (that is to say without contact) ; geometrically speaking it is a *projection*. In short, we have before us the equivalent of a rough sketch which has been shaded negatively.

Later on we will argue what name chemical science may give to this impression.

We propose now to go over our prints one by one in order to become thoroughly acquainted with them, and to see at the same time if they comply everywhere to the *law of distances*. In making this examination we must not lose sight of the fact that the linen cloth, far from being stretched, takes to a great extent the general shape of the various undulations which it passes over.

THE SHROUD OF CHRIST

Thus while the position of the impressions will often give us information as to the lie of the linen, on the other hand the linen lies on the body in conformity with natural laws. In short the image as it has been realized in these photographs must be anatomically correct, in spite of the distortions we have alluded to.

We will first take the print of the face and investigate the way in which it has been produced.

It is hardly necessary to recapitulate what we have demonstrated before as to the manner in which the cloth covered the head—it must have rested on something resembling a cushion placed on either side of the head : it did not touch the face lower than the cheek-bones, and was not near the ears, the neck, and the shoulders. We have already gone over this ground. It is the modelling of the different features of the face which we must study.

The cloth has rested firmly on the forehead, and its form is fairly plain, if we leave out of account a series of blotches, of which the meaning is still obscure.

On all the prints we find the same thing—marked and sudden darker or lighter tones on the figure. These are plainly connected with changes in the condition either of the body or of the linen. The fact that they are so marked gives strength to the theory of a natural impression, and lessens the probability of artistic production. Here we find no trace of handicraft, but ample evidence of the result of chance.

We shall not try to describe the way the hair is shown on the forehead ; certainly it is in the greatest disorder, and it is not easy to say what exact part of the print shows the forehead itself and what represents the hair, which must have left its impression at the same time as the forehead. The same applies to the traces of the moustache and beard.

For the same reason the arch of the eyebrows is only distinguished from the forehead by its progressive shading ; no one could trace the exact line of the eyebrows.

Immediately below the brows the distance between the linen and the face increases, and the circular hollows round the eyeballs were sufficiently deep to give but a very slight impression. This proves that chemical action decreased rapidly in proportion as the distance increased, and that it ceased when the distance was more than about one centimetre.

The eyeballs have produced a much fainter impression than the forehead or the cheek-bones ; but they are nevertheless quite discernible. It is easy to trace the line of each upper eyelid ; below this line the impression is weaker. The right eye seems quite shut ; the left eye, above which is the large drop of blood, has remained partially open.

The reproduction of the nose is really remarkable. A long nose, slightly aquiline and drooping towards the mouth, in fact the nose characteristic of Semitic races. The eyes are near together, which is another characteristic. The nose is not perfect—very narrow where it leaves the forehead, and just above the nostrils. It is greatly swollen in the middle portion, probably the result of a blow. The swelling which is on the left side of the nose has spread to the cheek, and is plainly visible on Plate III., where a light patch above a dark shadow corresponds to the swelling under the eye, the inner angle of which is clearly shadowed by it. On the right side of the face the modelling of the nose is quite different. Here a deep furrow extends from the corner of the eye vertically to the nostril.

Below the nose the moustache is strongly marked, though like the hair it is in disorder. To the right it seems to join the beard in surrounding the mouth, of which it covers the outer angle ; to the left it is raised and pressed against the cheek. It conceals the lines which we see as a rule between the cheek and the mouth.

There is nothing to say about the modelling of the left cheek ; clearly the cloth has not touched it, and the impression is very faint. There remains however a shadowy impression of the line below the cheek-bone ; on the left side the shading of the face is not normal as we have shown it to be on the right—indeed we come upon one of those flaws in the linen which seem to run through the whole length of the Shroud, and which do not seem capable of taking or preserving the impression. From this cause the modelling on the forehead seems suddenly interrupted.

The right cheek is clearly represented in all its details. To begin with, below the eye the cloth has pressed closely on the cheek-bone. More plainly than on the left side we see the hollow of the cheek under the cheek-bone, although part of the cheek itself is swollen, as we have shown, constituting the light line which falls obliquely from above the nostril to the region of the mouth. We see this condition occasionally in normal faces, and not infrequently with invalids. Perhaps this too may be the result of a blow. The cloth has here been in direct contact with the skin.

It is difficult to ascertain how the linen can have covered the mouth, which is clearly and admirably marked, the lower lip more distinctly than the upper. Doubtless the lower lip protruded more than the upper. This mouth is very striking. Very bitter and very proud at the same time, it gives to the whole head a deep look of sorrow, but sorrow devoid of anger.

Below the mouth the chin is well moulded, particularly on the left side ; the right side is disfigured by a blot, doubtless accidental, which in Plate No. III. produced the impression of a deep hollow. The cloth has rested closely on the chin, as on the forehead, on the nose, the cheek-bones, and the swollen portion of the right cheek. The modelling of the chin is interrupted by the transverse crease which was in the cloth when M. Pia took his photographs. Lower down there is a light patch, vaguely out-lined in Plate III. ; this is the result of a soil on the cloth, and not, as has been thought, the print of a long beard. The beard, on the contrary, has been kept short and almost square.

The modelling of the face calls for detailed study. Nothing here is symmetrical. If the left eyebrow is normal, the right is drawn down in the middle, rising again near the nose. The mouth and the moustache are slightly contorted, the mouth a little to the left of the facial axis, the left corner raised, the right lowered. We have already pointed out the irregularities in the nose. Here is none of the conventional regularity of feature common to pictures executed without a model, very far from the symmetry which an artist would give his picture, both because it would be easier, and because it would be more natural to do so. In proportion as we see more clearly the distance which separates this face from all pictorial art, the conviction that nature herself must have formed it grows upon us. The man we find here represented must have suffered greatly ; after His death His features must have remained unequally contracted.

Let us carefully study the print of the right side of the face between the forehead and chin. We have seen that the left side is marred by an accidental blot on the impression. We will take this opportunity of giving some passing geometrical observations in order to complete the general knowledge which we have of the impressions formed on the Shroud.

Below the cheek-bone the broken line which marks the outline of the print lightly touches the furrow which is marked underneath the cheekbone. Lower down the print gets narrower near the cheek, and wider again at the level of the beard. No doubt this is what would have happened naturally, as the linen did not cover all the face. But at first sight the shape of the face is disquieting to observers accustomed to see in a full face the bony outline on each side of the eyes; of this there is nothing, and consequently the upper portion of the head seems too narrow. Also in an ordinary portrait the ears tend to enlarge the surface which takes high light.

The cheek-bone and cheek are too strongly lighted, and so present more surface than they should, and come too far forward. In an ordinary drawing this portion would be shaded off in half tints.

The consequence is that on the Shroud the whole face, narrowed at the top and too equally lighted in the middle part, forms a sort of rectangle. But the eye soon gets accustomed to the curious modelling of the features, and finds the expression of the face very intense.

It is not difficult to demonstrate by a simple sketch the cause of these distortions. We will refer to figure 31 on this page. This drawing represents a transverse section of a face taken in the middle of the nose. Observe the linen cloth drooping from point O, passing near the cheekbones, and rising a little as it

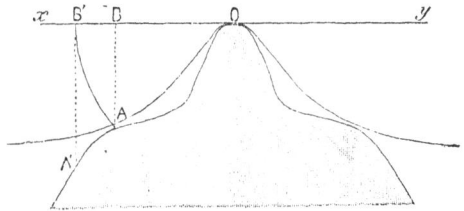

Fig. 31.

passes over the side-cushions already described It touches the front line of the nose, but is some distance from the sides. The strongest marking on the cheek-bone will be at point A.

THE SHROUD OF CHRIST

In this manner the cloth rested on the body, but for the observer it is now spread out flat, as shown at the line $x\,y$, and it is thus that we must consider the impressions.

It is easy to see that point A would not be represented where it is if the work were that of a painter. Instead of being projected to B, as we might expect to find, the A is reproduced at B'. In this way the part between A and the facial axis is enlarged. We must examine what actually is the point on the face represented by point B' on the Shroud ; unconsciously we refer it to A', of which B' is the projection, and not to point A. Now point A' has left no print on the Shroud—it is outside the zone of action ; nevertheless in a real face we should see the side perfectly, rather more in the shadow than A, and forming part of a receding plane. What, then, is the real distortion in the face, which must have been produced at the moment the print was made ? It consists in this—that the part of the subject which to our eye seems to correspond with A' is really a print of point A, which seems in stronger relief than it should be. The face however is still too narrow, as all that is projected on the plane $x\,y$ outside the line A' B' is left out in the image on the Shroud.

We may here present some theoretical considerations of a simple nature, which may be useful in understanding our subject.

How can a figure of undeniable artistic merit be produced by distant action ?

What conditions must this action fulfil in order to make such a result possible ?

Let us examine figure 32. Point A represents any point on the body. The cloth is represented by the line $x\,y$ at a given distance A B. On the cloth a series of points are represented by C D E, etc.

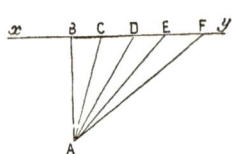

Let us suppose that the action diminishes very little in proportion to the increased distance—the chemical impression would be almost as strong at F as at B. If we assume that A F gives the distance at which the chemical action from point A would practically cease, we realize that the image of itself, projected by point A, would be in the nature of a circle of rays

Fig. 32.

142

IMPRESSIONS FROM SOME ACTION WITHOUT CONTACT

emanating from point A and striking the cloth at B F. The other points of the body would give off similar rays, and their circles would impinge on each other, producing as their result a very broken and confused image.

If, on the contrary, we suppose that the chemical action decreases very rapidly as the distance increases, the projection from A would be confined to the circles B D and the centre of this circle would be much more strongly marked than the part beyond.

This condition is represented on figure 32 by the mechanical thickening of the line $x\,y$, which increases from D to B. Under these conditions the rays from the different parts of the body would still impinge on each other, but in a much less degree than if they were stronger. The portrait would still resemble a badly focussed photograph, but would be more exact.

This is not all. If B A D represents an angle having its apex at A, and the sides A B A D, the length of the line B D must be reduced in proportion as A B is diminished. From this we demonstrate, that the shorter the distance at which point A ceases to give an impression on a sensitive surface, the clearer will be that impression ; the halo of the projection starting from a circle of rays, B D will diminish in ratio to the length A B, since it is the opening of the angle B A D, which limits the extent of the halo.

What do we conclude from the above argument ? This—that in order for a print produced without contact to be good the chemical action should cease very quickly as the distance increases. In the present case we see that this has been so, as the hollow round the eye, not a very deep one, is not marked on the cloth. A short consideration of figures 33 and 34 will complete our knowledge of the physical characteristics of these impressions.

In figure 33 the line A A' A'' refers to the surface of the body which is making its impression on the cloth, $x\,y$. So long as the body is parallel to the cloth from A to A' the image formed by it on the cloth has no cause to vary in intensity : it would be produced of a uniform tone. As soon as the emanating surface from A' to A''

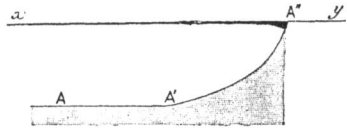

FIG. 33.

gets nearer the cloth, the intensity of its representation increases ; this we

143

indicate roughly in figure 33 by increasing the thickness of the line $x y$ in proportion as it approaches point A″, where the contact takes place. The point of contact corresponds to the point of least possible distance, and in consequence of greatest strength of effect produced.

In this manner the modelling of the face has been produced, and the same with the rest of the body. On the cloth, negative modelling has been formed which by a photographic process has now been restored to its positive.

But this is not all. Let us examine figure 34. Here we suppose that from A these emanations reach $x y$ at varying rates of speed. The surface A C makes a much more acute angle with the sensitive cloth than the surface A D. We have only to recall what we have seen in the last paragraph to recognize that the projection of A made at point B will represent the fainter impression of the whole right side C D. From B the impression will strengthen either towards C or towards D, but it will strengthen much more quickly towards D than towards C. At C and at D the intensity will be greatest as contact is realized at these two points—quickly between B and D, very slowly from B to C.

FIG. 34.

When we examine the photographic inversion of our impression in order to decipher its modelling we shall see that the plane which extends on the face from A to D seems to lose itself very quickly in the shadows starting from point D up to the most sunken zone situated at A. On the other hand C A vanishes much more slowly. Consequently the plane A D of the body seems in the shade, while the plane C A would seem to be in higher light.

Our reasoning would be similar if the geometrical position were reversed, that is to say if point A represented the point of contact and from this point the distance increased.

Let us apply this reasoning to the modelling of the eyes for instance.

On Plate III. the forehead seems in high light while the eyes are in shadow. This is because the eyebrows represent the point of contact, and the distance of the face from the cloth increases rapidly in proportion as the circular depression which surrounds the eyes is reached. For this reason the head seems lighted from above, although in reality it could receive no

IMPRESSIONS FROM SOME ACTION WITHOUT CONTACT

light at the moment of making its impression. It will be observed that with the mouth and chin also the light seems to come from above.

In figure 5 we find another interesting consequence of the geometrical laws which govern *impressions without contact*. Let us take A as the point of contact from which the cloth falls away little by little, following the direction of A A'. This is what happens when a rounded portion of the body rests on the under cloth, $x y$. The strength of the chemical impression will decrease indefinitely from the point A, ceasing altogether at A'. In other words, the contours of the figure will be lightly printed and will gradually

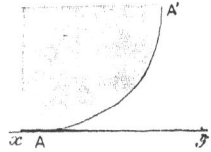

FIG. 35.

merge into the colourless cloth. We have shown that these are the conditions on the Holy Shroud.

The back imprint of the figure is shaded in exactly the same manner as the front ; we will illustrate our meaning by figure 36. Here we see the upper cloth, $x' y'$, resting gently on the body, sloping off gradually at the sides till it joins the under-cloth, $x y$. It will be remarked that the line $x' y'$ is the natural way in which a linen cloth would fall if allowed to follow the simple laws of weight and elasticity. We need no longer refer to geometry, but will try to glean some interesting facts from our impressions.

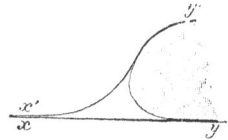

FIG. 36.

Let us suppose that parts of the body, differing from each other as do the skin and the beard, are yet possessed of the same chemical activity; these two parts would have their image projected on the sensitive cloth in conformity with the law of distance, no allowance being made for variation in colour. In other words, *colour does not exist* ; for the Shroud, nothing affects it but molecular action, in which colour takes no part. Inversely, when we find that two such different subjects as the skin and the beard give the same result at an equal distance, we conclude that their chemical activity must have been equal. As this is the result of our investigations as to the impression of the head on the Shroud, we must admit that the hair and the beard were under the same conditions as the skin.

It will be seen later on that we attribute the impressions on the Shroud

145

to the chemical action of the sweat, which must have drenched the head and beard as well as the face.

Consequently the impressions on the Shroud differ from any which either the human or photographic eye can have formed hitherto by means of the light radiated from every part of an ordinary subject. It is true that the print on the cloth *is* a negative, but, properly speaking, it is not a *photographic* negative—it is simply the inversion of the natural reliefs and hollows of the body. The positive photograph of this impression only restores the nature of these reliefs ; it could not give a scale of colour which the print itself does not give. For this reason (the absence of any colour-effect) the impressions are not shaded any more than if they were taken from a statue or moulding, instead of from a human body, which from all the details given above we may now assume that it was.

There is no reason to be surprised that the beard and moustache as shown in Plate III. appear white in places which are strongly printed. The impression will give us no information as to whether the man it represents was fair or dark, and we have no means of solving this question.

We will now continue our investigations. We have fully examined the head ; we must now see how the rest of the body has produced its impression on the cloth.

Let us survey the front image from head to feet. We have already noticed that the shoulders are absent, that the breasts are strongly marked, leaving a fainter trace, as would be natural, along the centre line of the thorax, and projecting enough to have made the cloth lose contact with the body just beneath them. The contact has been renewed almost immediately, and shows the gastric and abdominal regions. Laterally the cloth rests on the arms ; between these and the body there was of course a deep hollow. The umbilical mark can be faintly distinguished. On Plate V it may be noticed as a faint ring with a dark circle round it ; this forms the centre of a well-developed part of the figure, shown with the forearms on either side.

Below this the abdomen is depressed and the hands are crossed below it.

The forearms are reduced to a narrow band, below which, near the wrists, the edge of the pelvis may just be distinguished in the shadows. There seems reason to question whether rolls of linen or other supports have not been placed on either side of the body in the region of the fore-arms in the same manner as would appear to have been done for the head.

If the upper cloth had been free to follow the law of its own weight, it must have covered the arms and have rested on the hips.

Further, M. Gazet, who conducted the researches in the tombs at Faijum, assures me that accessory pieces of linen, rolled up to keep the body in place, are always presumable when an Eastern entombment is under consideration.

Whatever may be the reason, it is clear that the linen did not cover the arms in the same way as it did the wrists. The representation of the fore-arms on the Shroud is quite different to anything that a painter would have given. The left hand rests on the right in a most natural manner. Any one can make the experiment by lying on his back and advancing the forearms as he clasps his hands. They will fall naturally into the position shown on the Shroud. Four fingers of the left hand are visible ; the thumb seems turned under ; the beginning of the fingers is perfectly plain—the divisions between them form three dark lines (Plate v.). The right hand, which is underneath, is hardly seen ; the fingers of this hand have given no detailed impression, but are only distinguished by a general shadow cut by the creases in the cloth. These creases are perpendicular to the axis of the body. They were there when the photograph was taken, for they extend down the entire length of the cloth.

The right thigh is hardly visible, while the left is strongly marked on the outside edge. We best discern the line of the outer muscle, more plainly indicated as it gets nearer to the knee, which is very clearly marked. If the legs had been placed quite symmetrically, or rather if the cloth had touched them equally, it should have rested on this part of the body, as shown in figure 37A by a transverse section taken through the lower part of the thighs. We must bear in mind that the construction of the body is correct as a whole in spite of the accidental causes, chemical or other, which may have disturbed its normal condition.

Between the thighs there would be a marked hollow, such as our sketch shows in the shape of a V. The cloth must therefore have been far above the inner region of the thighs and the adductor muscles. In the impression there is moreover a line stretching from the hands and becoming narrower towards the knees, where the linen has received no impression. The knees were touching each other, but in the hollow round the kneecap there remained also an interval of non-impression.

The left kneecap only is well marked, as was also the left thigh. The region of the calves, which were enveloped and thus enlarged, is marked with great exactness. We have no difficulty in seeing their form ; the modelling here is the reverse of that on the thighs, as we shall explain in figure 37B. It is plain that there is a certain space between the highest point and the two tibias, and the cloth could not fail to fall sideways along the muscles of the legs ; also at the indication of the muscle of the foreleg the impression is stronger —this prominent place is separated from the knee by a slight depression. Laterally the cloth remained in contact with the body till it passed the corresponding outer muscle of the calf of the leg. Thus, while the section of the thighs at A may be roughly represented by a V, the

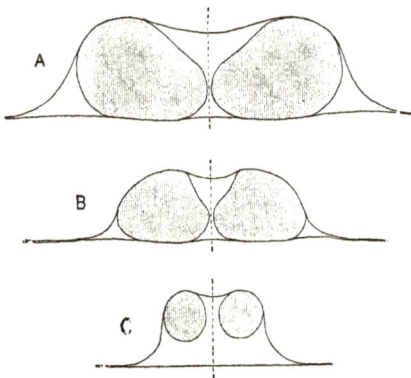

Fig. 37.

section at the calves of the leg may be described as a wide open A with extended sides. Immediately below the calves the print gets narrower and weaker. From this point the figure becomes altogether vague without quite disappearing from the cloth. We may well assert that this rendering of the thighs and calves is most unlike the manner in which a painter would have represented them. But this observation applies even more to the region of the ankles.

To explain how the ankles with their slender section are represented by a wide band of printing, we must assume that here the cloth must have touched the body as shown in figure 37 at c, where the wrapping must have been closer than elsewhere. The ankles (as we shall show later on) are considerably raised above the level of the under-cloth, so that the upper cloth may have fallen naturally closely over their sides. There could be no thought of special pictorial arrangement on the part of the person who placed the cloth over the body.

It is asked at what point we cease to be able to examine the front impression on M. Pia's photograph. Figure 38 will answer this question. The outline of the leg is cut by the dotted line L a. We will explain how we have been able to define this limit so accurately. The front impression is cut off a little below the ankle, as shown on Plates IV. and V., the feet on the Shroud having been folded back under the frame at the time of M. Pia's photograph. The impression, a little below the ankles, though still some-what vague, begins to get stronger, and it would seem that the contact, almost lost below the calf of the leg, will give good results when it approaches the feet, as shown in figure 38.

We will now study the impression of the back of the figure.

The back of the head gives a strong imprint. The hair is quite distinct ; it is long, and covers the head and neck, spreading down to the shoulder-blades. In M. Pia's proofs even the locks of hair are admirably perceptible ; in printing they have somewhat lost their distinctness.

The shoulders, shown on either side of the mass of hair, are rather high. It must be remembered that they rest firmly on the cloth, which must have pressed against them, but the over-development is not excessive.

The left shoulder-blade is more strongly indicated than the right, but both project and are strongly marked on the cloth. Below them the thorax is well modelled, but the outline fades away on each side. It gets weaker also at the spine near its base, and where the back curves away from the cloth the impression almost disappears. At this point there are traces of water-stains on the cloth, which cross the central line in a narrow and sinuous belt.

Lower still the form of the sacrum is visible where the weight of the body rests on the fleshy part of the back. After this there is again a gap in the impression, which reappears at the thighs, the left side being again the more clearly marked.

THE SHROUD OF CHRIST

The hollows under the knees are clearly distinguished ; so are the calves of the legs—from this point the impression grows fainter down to the level of the tendon Achilles. These tendons must have been raised perceptibly above the level of the lower cloth. The reason for this is not far to seek— the feet are pressed downward and the heels are pressed backwards towards the calves, as shown in figure 38.

If the feet had maintained their normal condition they would have shown an angle of about 80° with the axis of the body ; the heels would have been in their natural place, and the tendon Achilles would have rested against the lower cloth.

After studying this impression of the back of the body we wished to be assured that the indications shown were anatomically correct. For this purpose one of our friends kindly laid down on the table in the laboratory in a similar position to that shown on the Shroud. Under these conditions the weight of the body rests on the back of the head, the shoulder-blades, the fleshy parts of the back, the calves of the legs, and on the heels. The thighs barely touch the table ; it is easy to slip the hand under them. No doubt they are not far from the cloth, but they do not press upon it, as the calves of the legs have evidently done. For this reason, then, the impression of the thighs, though distinct, is very faint. The lumbar region and the tendon Achilles are raised as in the figure on the Shroud. The above will show that the impression of the back of a body on the Shroud is strictly realistic. One point only remains unexplained. How have the soles of the feet, and particularly of the right foot, made an impression though they are so distant from the horizontal plane ?

There are many possible reasons for this—rolls of linen may have been placed under the cloth to support the feet, the lower cloth may have been turned up to cover the feet. It is impossible to say with any certainty. What we have observed is sufficient to prove absolutely that the impression is perfectly natural.

We will proceed to explain what is the meaning of figure 38.

We placed on the photographic plate, a sheet of paper, in such a manner that its edge was parallel to the axis of the figure, and showed clearly the impress of the legs. We produced from this line a series of perpendicular lines passing through the most definite points of the body. The first perpendicular gives the edge of the photograph L p ; a second marks the projection of the right heel, which is plainly shown ; then with great care we were able to distinguish the outline of the calves, the hollow under the knee, the furrow which lies between the thighs and the fleshy part of the back ; finally we were able to follow the modelling of the sacrum and the lumbar region, thus gradually and carefully tracing the outline of the hip and leg. After this, taking careful measurements, we corrected the front view by the back view of the figure, and completed the outline of the foot.

This done we turned the photographs in such a manner as to bring our sheet of paper on a line with the front view and its edges parallel to the

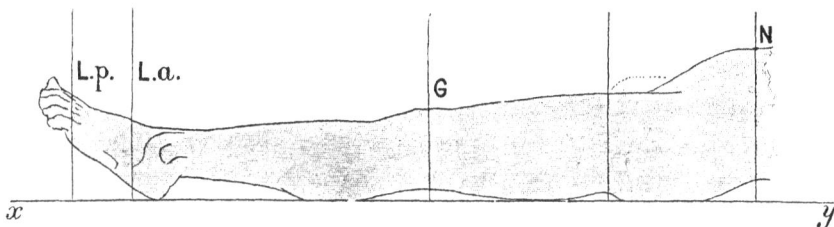

FIG. 38.

central line of the cloth. We placed the sheet of paper so that a perpendicular line drawn from the centre of the left kneecap fell at point G, and found that the front outline of the leg was in its right place on the paper. We proceeded to mark at L a, not exactly the edge of the photograph, but the point at which the image on it ceased to be visible. We then ascertained that the muscles of the leg were rightly placed on the photograph, and that the representations of the back and front of a body corresponded with perfect exactness.

It was by tracing a line from the small of the back to the front that we discovered the marks of the umbilicus. We were not looking for it, not having before noticed it on the photographs. After this we reduced our sketch, to bring it to the same scale as the prints from the photographs. It remained to ascertain if the length of the legs was normal. We know that when a man stands upright, the distance from the ground to the kneecap measures twice the length of the head. Taking the length from the inside angle of the eye to the lower edge of the chin, in M. Pia's photograph, this gives us from 1 cm. to 1 cm. 8 mm. The double of this, 3 cm. 5 mm., gives the length of the head. Twice this again is 7 cm. Now from the centre of the left kneecap to the level which would be occupied by the sole of the foot, if the foot were placed perpendicular to the axis of the body, would be about 7 cm. 2 mm. The length of the leg is then absolutely correct.

In making the calculations necessary to ascertain the length of the body in relation to the head we find that the length of the head is multiplied 7·2 times. But our calculations are not sufficiently exact to insist on this point. There is a slight uncertainty in measuring the head which, according to the scale in M. Pia's studies, would make a considerable modification in the final result.

In such cases the eye is the best judge, and for any one accustomed to drawing it is evident that the body represented on the Holy Shroud is in perfect proportion. In spite of the vagueness of the contours and the deformation by enlargement or diminution, resulting from the different degrees of contact, we may even go so far as to say that there is a certain nobility about it. Looking at M. Pia's negative of the back view of the figure placed upright, it needs no very strong imagination to picture it as the representation of a solidly modelled statue, seen in half light. We might almost think that if the light could be intensified the statue would stand out with complete reality.

We wish to conclude this long chapter with the word reality. Little by little we have banished all side issues, we have presented the precise terms of our problem, and we have described the physical characteristics of the impressions.

If we reduce the question to its logical issue, we can now affirm positively that we have here no painting, but genuine impressions subject to natural laws of distance and contact. The subject is fraught with difficulties and complexities, but we do not hesitate to assert that the

impressions on the Shroud at Turin are the result of a natural phenomenon.

We must ascertain in the next chapter what are the chemical and
other conditions which can have produced this phenomenon.

CHAPTER VII

EXPERIMENTAL RESEARCHES AS TO NEGATIVE IMPRESSIONS RESULTING FROM CHEMICAL ACTION WITHOUT CONTACT

THE impressions on the Holy Shroud are produced by chemical action, largely without absolute contact between the body and the cloth. Of this we have no doubt. We shall now try to produce similar prints.

When we wish to produce delicately shaded pictures by chemical action it is natural to apply first to photography with its sensitive plates. Therefore it is with a photographic plate that we shall first seek to demonstrate the working of the physical law of actions where the active body and the receptive surface are not in contact. Later we shall endeavour to reproduce as closely as possible the conditions under which the impressions on the Shroud were actually formed.

We have already stated in the Introduction how deeply we are indebted to M. Colson, Professor of Physics at the École Polytechnique, for his invaluable help in our investigations.

I

M. le Commandant Colson published in 1900 [1] a very comprehensive review of " the manner in which photographic films may be influenced by distant objects." Any one wishing for information on this subject would do well to read this article, but we will now only inquire from M. Colson as to the general appearance of these phenomena and the manner in which they may be classified. Here we cannot do better than quote his own words : " The actions taking place between substances more or less separated from each other can be divided into two distinct classes. Those produced by *radiation* (that is to say by a sort of vibratory move-

[1] See *Bulletin de la Société Française de Photographie*, vol. xiv. pp. 481–90.

ment, the source which acts dynamically on the sensitive plate), and those produced by *gases* or *vapours* which emanate from certain substances and act chemically on the sensitive plate. It is not difficult to distinguish between these two methods of action. Radiation is transmitted through any given medium in a straight line through certain substances even of close texture and may present the same phenomena in reflection, refraction, defraction, and polarization as in the case of light ; whereas gases and vapours diffuse in air, and only penetrate porous substances."

In addition to the well known Röntgen rays, action due to radiation may be caused by electric or luminous phenomena. Light produced by the electric arc, by aluminium, or by magnesium will influence a sensitive film through paper, cardboard, or even wood. Much attention is being given at the present time to substances which are specifically radio-active such as *uranium, theorium, polonium*, the famous *radium* discovered by M. and Madame Curie, also various compounds of *barium* specially studied by M. Bela von Lengyel. These various metals and their salts can produce radiation without the addition of any external stimulus.

As it seems hardly possible that a human body should become, or be capable of becoming, properly speaking, radio-active, we will not concern ourselves with phenomena of this sort, in our endeavour to account for the impressions on the Holy Shroud.

By employing gases or vapours we shall approach more nearly to natural conditions.

We have to go as far back as 1816 to find, in Nicephore Niepce, the first observer who endeavoured to affect a sensitive plate by the action of vapours. These researches have never been quite abandoned. We need not detail them as our concern is not with the history of the question.

We were so fortunate as to be put into communication with M. Colson just at the time when we first began our inquiry as to the effects of vapours produced by all sorts of essences and resins, as demonstrated by Russell in his paper[1] " on the action exerted by certain metals and other substances on a photographic plate." M. Colson urged us to try the action

[1] *Proceedings Royal Society*, lxi. pp. 424-33.

of zinc vapour to begin with. He was the first to experiment with zinc vapour, the activity of which is considerable, in 1896, so we will quote from his own account of these experiments, written in 1900.

" A thin plate of zinc, rubbed bright with emery paper, if placed in the dark room on a gelatinous bromide plate, will produce upon it an effect which after the action of a developer manifests itself by a tint of dark grey. To produce this action it is not necessary previously to expose the metal to the rays of the sun.

" The action is strong, and the grey tint is produced in a few hours, even at a distance of several centimetres. It passes through paper, thin cardboard, thin wood, albumen, gelatine, and porous bodies generally, and passes round obstacles; compact substances such as glass, metal, gums and crystallized substances interfere with its direct passage. The numerous experiments which I have made establish that this action is not a radiation such as occurs from radio-active substances, but is caused by the disengagement of zinc vapour . . . which ceases directly the surface of the metal has become oxidized by the moisture of the atmosphere. I have established the same property in magnesium and cadmium, but have failed with mercury, doubtless because it does not diffuse easily in gelatine." The vapour really accumulates in the gelatine film and remains there inert till the plate is being developed. " At this point," says M. Colson, " the particles of metal in an excessively fine state of division which form the vapour, are oxidized by the action of water and the developer, and bring about the reduction of the bromide ; the oxidation of the particles of zinc is hastened by the fact that in contact with the molecules of bromide they form the oxidisable element in an infinity of little electric couples, which become increasingly active in proportion as the silver returns to its metallic form, until all the immeshed vapour is exhausted." M. Colson established the fact that it was a question of emanation and not of radiation; what proves that the vapour was really diffused is that it passed round obstacles in its way.

Further, M. Colson convinced himself that the effect was due to zinc, and not to any constituent of the air, the results being the same when worked in vacuo.

RESEARCHES AS TO NEGATIVE IMPRESSIONS

In these experiments, as in others where active substances have been made to reach on sensitive surfaces without the intervention of any optical instrument, there was no thought of obtaining modelled pictures or indeed pictures of any sort. Further, the conditions of these phenomena did not seem favourable to the representation, however rough, of the modelling of any object. These vapours, which, M. Colson tells us, have great power of diffusion and can go round objects, would seem far less suitable for giving details, than radiation, which at least travels in direct lines ; and in this respect granting that their activity decreases sufficiently in proportion as the distance increases, they seem to be more manageable than vapour for the production of negative.

We give another quotation from M. Colson showing how difficult it is to regulate vapour. " A plate shut in a box for forty-eight hours with a piece of bright zinc placed in such a manner that its vapour shall act on the plate (not directly but by diffusion from a distance through the air) will show a distinct fog, except on those portions of the plate which are protected by the immediate contact of a non-porous body." Again he says : " I placed on the sensitive plate a little piece of sheet zinc bent at a right angle, one half lying horizontally on the plate, the other standing at right angles. Opposite this upright portion, at a distance of three millimetres, I placed a vertical sheet of cardboard pierced by an opening which started from the level of the plate. If there had been any question of radiation there should have been shown on the plate a trace of the opening with its shadow, according to the geometrical laws of radiation. Nothing of the sort was produced ; a *shaded grey tint* extended from the zinc not only on the inside of the opening but all over the piece of cardboard except on the place where it rested on the plate. In another experiment I placed the zinc on a sort of cardboard bridge six millimetres high ; *a shaded tint* of grey spread all over it, and even underneath. In this experiment, as in many others, *it went round the obstacle,* proving it to be the effect *not of a radiation but of an emanation.*"

We have italicised the words *shaded tint* as this remark of M. Colson is the only one up to the present which tends to bring us near the conditions observed in the impressions on the Shroud.

In his first memoir Russell alludes to rather more precise actions.

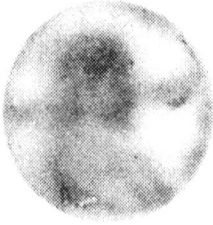

Facsimile of the
chemical impression.

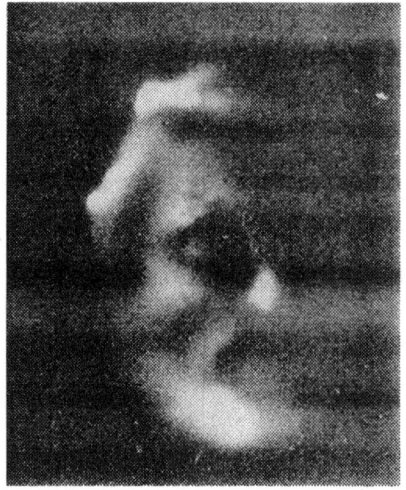

Silver medal, belonging to
M. Boyer d'Agen, and reputed
to be of the XVIth century :
Called " Medaille du Campo dei fiori "

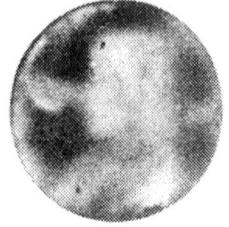

Photographic inversion
of the chemical impression.

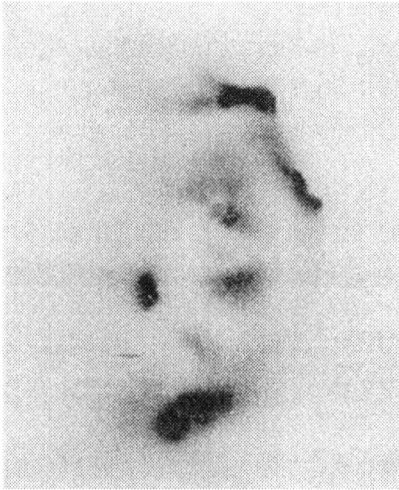

Chemical impression.

Photographic inversion of the chemical impression.

Head of Christ (plaster mould).

IMPRESSIONS PRODUCED BY CHEMICAL ACTION.

THE SHROUD OF CHRIST

He specifies that if a piece of zinc is placed in contact with a photographic plate any lines or marks visible on the zinc will be reproduced on the sensitive film. This remark proves that if the actions are in no way directed they at least vary fairly rapidly when the distance increases but slightly. In any case Russell has not reproduced the reliefs of an object from the point of view of a veritable model.

As an example of the reproduction of an object in relief we may cite the Moser images produced in the following manner. Rub with the fingers, or warm slightly, a copper medal ; place it on a plate of polished silver; remove the medal and project either steam or vapour of mercury on the silver plate. These vapours condense unequally, and there appears on the plate the image of the copper medal. But these conditions are not those of the impressions on the Holy Shroud.

And yet if the authors of the experiments cited have failed to obtain impressions similar to those on the Shroud it is only because their researches have not led them in the same direction. We shall demonstrate that impressions can be modelled in negative with the greatest simplicity.

However this may be, it will be seen that it is not from experiments hitherto made in the laboratory that we have discovered the physical laws of the impressions on the Shroud. On the contrary, it is the direct study of the impressions which has led us to attribute them to an action taking place between substances separated from each other, and we start now from this direct study in our endeavour to reproduce similar images by some simple method.

M. Colson and I decided that we should both employ objects of well defined form for our experiments, but should vary the conditions sufficiently for our researches to be mutually complementary.

M. Colson made a plaster mould about ten centimetres high from a head of Christ. He preferred plaster as he had found it possible to make a small quantity of newly prepared powdered zinc adhere to it by friction. After charging the plaster with this active substance he placed it on a Lumière plate *marque bleue*, gelatine side up, in a light tight box. The object only touched the gelatine at three points, and, if one may

158

RESEARCHES AS TO NEGATIVE IMPRESSIONS

use the expression, the photographic plate *saw* a three-quarter view of the head. Forty-eight hours later M. Colson developed the plate, which we reproduce at the lower left-hand corner of Plate VIII. This impression is the homologue, not chemical but physical, of the impressions on the Holy Shroud. It is a true negative impression. The crown of thorns, the lower part of the nose and of the chin, which is covered by the beard, were in actual contact with the sensitive film ; these parts have produced a very strong impression. The forehead, the cheek-bones, the moustache, and the eyeball, were at further and various degrees of distance. These parts have marked the plate unequally, the forehead and the cheekbone being better developed than the eye or the moustache. The left part of the forehead and the middle part of the beard are only half visible as they gradually recede, fading away in the shadows. The modelling comes out well, the arch of the eyebrow being particularly noticeable. The head has the same appearance of being lighted from above, as we have already remarked in the impressions on the Shroud.

Let us proceed to invert this image by means of photography, simply taking by contact a *phototype* of the plate. We thus obtain a positive impression, which may be seen to the right of the direct print on Plate VIII. This reproduces the object as it would have appeared if viewed from the position of the sensitive plate, reconstructing the projection of the little head as an artist might have sketched it, the relief being represented by the natural effects of light and shade. This illustration on the right is then the equivalent of the negative plates of the Shroud. In other words it is the homologue of our Plates III. and V. Here is the same absence of precise contours, the same suggestion of an actual form rather than a picture. The image obtained by zinc has greater depth than the print on the Shroud, because the homogeneity of the sensitive gelatine spread over a glass plate would be more perfect than that of any receptive substance spread, perhaps irregularly, on a cloth. In the same way the small plaster head rubbed over with zinc would have more equal emissive power than the human head, the activity from which is without doubt due to some physiological phenomena necessarily subject to accidental variations. Also the plate taken by M. Colson is quite intact, whereas the

159

linen at Turin, even if its date is taken as the fourteenth century, has suffered from the wear of time.[1]

M. Colson having selected a subject with high reliefs for his experiments, I preferred for mine to take a small medal, on which the maximum relief did not exceed one or two millimetres. In M. Colson's cast the features being broadly modelled, would naturally give a definite result; in my own experiment I did not expect to get a detailed outline of the figures on the medal, some of which were very small, and others removed from the plate by a distance greater than their own dimensions. Still it was interesting to determine the sensitiveness of the method by ascertaining the result which chemical action could produce under such unfavourable conditions. The print obtained was extraordinarily faithful, in spite of the anticipated drawbacks.

I selected for my purpose the medal of M. Boyer of Agen, published by Falaizi & Co. It is not because I think of giving it an exceptional archaeological importance, nor that I protest against the opinion of those who assign it to the sixteenth century. This question is outside my subject. But the modelling on this medal is both simple and strong, and the relative proportions of the reliefs suited my plan.

The results of my efforts appear in the upper part of Plate VIII., on either side of the normal photograph of the medal. To the left is the negative; to the right is the positive, resulting from the inversion thereof.

The medal being of silver, I sprayed it with fine zinc powder, freshly prepared. With a sable brush I removed all the powder which had fallen on the flat part of the medal; by so doing, while operating on an object in low relief, I simulated the action which would be produced by an object in repoussé, of which the edges would be unequally removed from the receptive surface. I left a little zinc powder on the lettering of the medal, and also on the outside edge, in order to frame the image. This done I placed face

---

[1] The head on the Holy Shroud and our experimental print must not be compared together from the point of view of the modelling of the various features of the face. The one was seen from the front and was on supple cloth the other was a three-quarter view on a rigid plate. For example the mouth is very well defined on the Shroud, whilst in M. Colson's experiment it is a long distance from the receptive plate.

downwards over the medal a " Lumière " plate " marque bleue." It rested on props of cardboard, placed on each side of the medal, and actually touched the forehead and left shoulder, as may be perceived in examining these phototype prints. At the end of twenty-four hours I developed the plate and obtained quite a satisfactory result. The details of the outline are not there, but the scale of relief is quite in order. The waves in the hair are quite perceptible, also the folds of the drapery. The sensitive plate recorded even slight gradations, as may be seen in examining the medal. In addition to this the intensity of the emanation decreased so rapidly when the distance increased, that the hollow of the neck, or the slope of the right shoulder, are more distinct than in the photograph itself. Doubtless the photograph gives details which the print made without a lens cannot distinguish, but on the other hand the photograph is in error with regard to relative relief. For instance, in the photograph taken through a lens we might think that the right shoulder projects almost as far as the left, and that the chin makes but a very slight projection from the neck. The chemical impression on the contrary tends rather to exaggerate the variations of the active surface, and on our print, far from perceiving a mere flat representation, we obtain an impression in marked relief.[1]

In order to avoid all confusion in our analogy between our experimental prints and those on the Holy Shroud, we will place side by side in two columns all the conditions which refer to them, in order that they may be more easy to compare.

CONDITIONS OF THE SHROUD	EXPERIMENTS MADE WITH ZINC
I. The emissive object is a human body.	I. The emissive object acts in virtue of the zinc which covers its surface.
II. The receptive surface is a fabric on which appears an impression modelled in negative.	II. The receptive surface is a photographic plate; the impression on it is modelled in negative.
III. In order to get the true modelling of the body it is necessary to photograph the cloth with a lens and examine the sensitive plate after development. In other words, this negative, as it would be called from the photographic standpoint, is truly a positive rendering from the impressions on the Shroud.	III. In order to obtain the true modelling as the print is made on a glass plate it will be enough to print from it on sensitive paper, which will then show a positive or correct view of the subject.

[1] We must here note an important difference between M. Colson's experiment and mine.

THE SHROUD OF CHRIST

It is obvious that if the order in which these actions were produced was not definitely stated, if any one of the stages of the chemical action was not clearly recognized and defined, hopeless confusion would result.

The law of distances, which is manifest in the impressions on the Shroud, is evidently applicable to the vapours given off by the zinc at an ordinary temperature. The negative prints which resulted from the action of these vapours are much more accurate than might have been expected. The rendering of the relief is both strong and delicate. Doubtless there are many objects which it would be impossible to reproduce in this way, and the applications of the method are necessarily restricted. With a firm surface like the plate of glass, or even a partially flexible surface, such as a gelatine film, we can only reproduce objects in which the principal reliefs approach a common plane, and the hollows do not exceed about a centimetre in depth. Nevertheless, certain objects, principally very flat bas-reliefs reproduced in this manner, would give very fine pictures, which would not be without a mysterious charm.

The important point to note is that the above experiments need not be restricted to vapour from zinc ; any vapour given out sufficiently slowly and regularly in a quiet atmosphere for a long enough time must distribute itself round the object from which it emanates, in concentric zones of rapidly decreasing density.

Under these conditions, if these vapours strike against a suitable surface they will always form an image something similar to the one obtained by zinc. We may then hope to arrive at chemical conditions analogous to those by which the impressions on the Holy Shroud were produced, now that we know precisely how much to expect as to the facility with which we can imitate the physical characteristics of these impressions.

II

We will now inquire what are the conditions necessary before a human body, alive or dead, can leave an impression on a cloth which

M. Colson made his zinc vapour act from above downwards, the object resting on the plate ; I made it act from below upwards. We have shown that the result in both cases was successful.

is in accordance with the law of distances. It would be necessary not only that the body should emit these vapours slowly and with regularity, but also the cloth would need to be specially prepared in order to be rendered sensitive to these vapours, so that its original colour would be sensibly modified. A simple linen cloth would fulfil the conditions if carefully prepared with a suitable substance.

Here then is our whole problem, and to solve it we must try to find some clue which may enable us to form a provisional hypothesis.

The Holy Shroud is said to have been brought from the East. À priori nothing seems to prove this assertion, but we may provisionally accept it as true for the sake of our argument.

Tradition is said to have been even more explicit : it claims that this is the true Shroud of Christ. We must rigorously investigate this tradition. We know that this cloth has certainly covered the body of a man, and that it has retained from this man's body an imprint which is conformable to the law of distances. To advance further we must have recourse to an hypothesis, to give weight to Traditional Belief.

We learn then from history that amongst Orientals, and particularly among the Jews, it was the habit to employ aromatic substances, specially myrrh and aloes, in burial. If this is a fact it is possible that these substances may have helped to produce these impressions—the body or the cloth, or both, may have been covered with spices.

In employing these substances, gums, resins, etc., of a brown colour, they pounded them up with olive oil so as to form a sort of unguent.

M. Colson, who is as careful as an antiquarian as he is learned as a physician, studied in the Old Testament the methods prescribed by Moses relative to the preparation of the perfumes used for anointing the tabernacle and the holy vessels consecrated to its service. For this service, as for feeding the lamps in the Temple, only pure oil made from olives which had been pounded in a mortar could be used. And it is this sacred oil which " ran down Aaron's beard, even to the skirts of his garment " (Lev. ch. viii.).

M. Gayet, whose work I have already referred to, has shown me all sorts of shrouds found in the Egyptian tombs. In some cases the mummy has left vague imprints on the enveloping cloth like a brown stain equally devoid of shape and gradation. I have thought I recognized the print of a back, but no distinct shape was visible. M. Gayet was good enough to give me the Egyptian shroud on which this brown shading was perceptible. Perhaps some day it may serve to prove that there is no resemblance between the mark on this coarse outer casing and the print at Turin, which is equivalent to a portrait. There is no possible resemblance between the stains caused by partial decomposition and the picture produced by natural laws.[1]

The unguent formed from myrrh and aloes mixed with oil, the Greek μίγμα, was semi-fluid, and as used in burial it constituted a not very efficacious preservative against decomposition.

Let us suppose that the body whose impression on the Shroud we are considering had been wrapped in a linen cloth smeared with a mixture of myrrh and aloes. We are not here dealing with a body mummified in the Egyptian manner as a glance at the figures on the cloth shows. The numerous traces of wounds thereon prove that the body had been neither washed nor prepared in the elaborate method employed by the Egyptians. It is enough to observe with what delicacy the features, particularly the eyes and lips, have left their imprint, to be sure that no bandages were interposed between the Shroud and the body. The cloth has not been tied anywhere. It would seem that if the intention had been to bury the body the preliminaries had been done hastily and in an unfinished manner. This would be incompatible with Egyptian rites. We say that the naked body was placed under this cloth ; where then were the unguents placed ?

Are we to think that the body was covered by the mixture and that the aromatic spices acted by their vapours on the cloth ? But how then was the cloth made sensitive ?

If we admit that the spices covered both body and cloth, then both surfaces, being chemically equivalent, would not react on each other.

Only one hypothesis is possible—the unguents were spread on the cloth, thus rendering it sensitive to the action of the organic emanations from the body.

[1] *Recueil d'études historiques, Consacrées à la memoire de Bela III., roi de Hongrie,* 1173-- 1196, by T. de Forster, Buda Pesth, 1900. See p. 275, fig. 186 ; and p. 277, fig. 187.

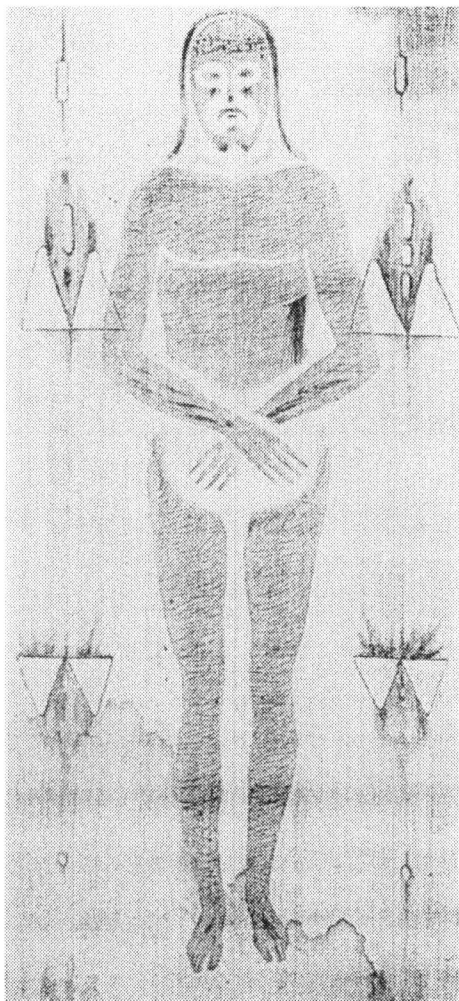

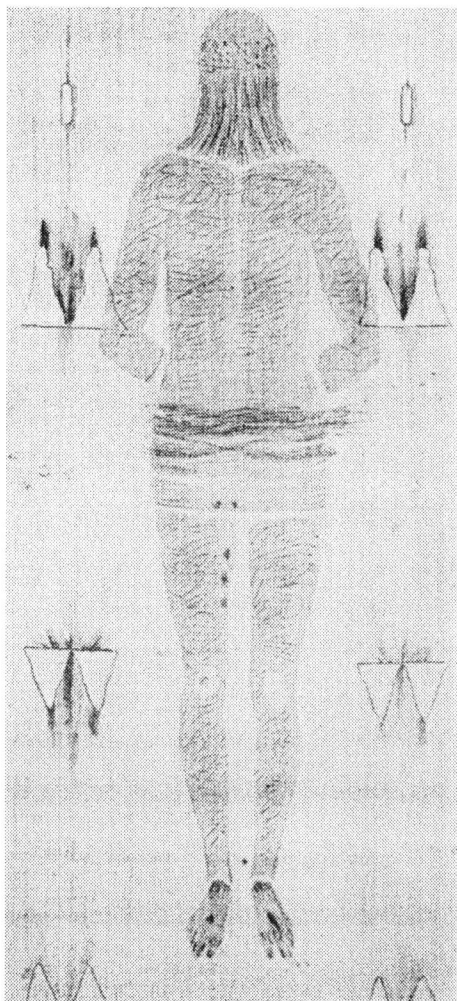

COPY OF THE HOLY SHROUD

as shown in a water colour drawing in sepia, painted on cloth, preserved in the church of Notre-Dame de Chambéry.

RESEARCHES AS TO NEGATIVE IMPRESSIONS

All will go well if we can discover what sort of organic vapours the body could give out which would act on a mixture of myrrh and aloes in such a way as to modify their colour in accordance with the law of distances and so produce negative impressions. M. Colson has made this discovery.

Aloes contain two chemical principles—one is aloin, which added to water gives a pale yellow solution and is darkened by alkalies ; the other is aloetine, which oxidizes readily, particularly with alkalies, and forms a brown substance.[1]

Knowing the properties of aloetine, M. Colson considered whether it might not be possible under certain conditions for a human body to emit alkaline vapours which should diffuse themselves round the body and react on the mixture of aloes at a distance according to the law of negative prints.

It was necessary to try experiments in order to appreciate the practical value of this idea. In the first place, do ammoniacal vapours act in a manner comparable with those of zinc, and secondly, is a human body under any given conditions capable of emitting ammoniacal vapours ? M. Colson and I have devoted ourselves to solving these questions.

To begin with, it was necessary to ascertain whether ammoniacal vapours would darken the colour on a cloth soaked in a mixture of oil and aloes, and it was so. The darkening took place slowly or quickly, according to the amount of the vapour to which it was exposed.

Further, M. Colson discovered that in the parts thus darkened the mixture became firmly fixed on the cloth. So long as no chemical transformation took place, the oil merely held the powdered aloes in suspension. If the cloth were brushed almost all the aromatic particles disappeared ; on the other hand, as soon as oxidation took place the oil became modified, producing with the darkened aloes a semi-solid, permanently encrusted in the texture of the linen. The cloth remained perfectly supple, and the colouring matter constituted either a flexible incrustation or a simple dye, according as the oil was more or less loaded with the aloes. There are aloes of different colours ; the powder varies from yellow to a red-brown.

[1] *Dictionnaire de chimie de Würtz*, the article on aloes.

An ordinary mixture gives the cloth a light yellow tint. After oxidation the parts which have been exposed to ammoniacal vapours differ greatly from those which have remained intact ; the colour of the oxidized regions varies in the same proportion as the colour of the pure resin used in the operation.[1]

To sum up, we are convinced that a linen cloth which had been saturated with oil and aloes would, after a lapse of years, or rather centuries, look like an ordinary cloth *except in those parts where* it had been subjected to the action of ammoniacal vapours. In these parts it would be covered with blotches, varying in intensity, more or less shaded at the edges, the colour of rust, or rather resembling blood-stains. And this, we must remember, is the aspect presented by the Holy Shroud.

M. Colson and I, encouraged by our first favourable results, sought further to discover if the ammoniacal vapours acting on the preparation of aloes obeyed the law of distances—in other words, we tried to produce with them negative impressions.

Our manner of working may seem simple, but was in fact a very delicate operation. In order to find an object in relief the surface of which should be capable of giving out moist ammoniacal vapours we took a plaster cast and saturated it with ammoniacal water. Ammonia from this is given off little by little. At first it was given off too fast, and only a general brown blur was obtained; then if the plaster was very wet it saturated the linen when it touched the cast. At these points, instead of the darkest tints, which might be expected, it produced yellow blotches with brown edges. Round these blotches the oxidation took place by the action of the vapour, but the general modelling was destroyed. If however the plaster was too dry, then the contrary action was seen—the oil penetrated the plaster and stopped up the pores, thus preventing the evaporation of the ammonia, and no oxidized impression was produced.

[1] An ammoniacal solution colours the linen sensitized with aloes just as the vapours do. Solutions of alkaline carbonates do the same. The presence of oil is not necessary for the colouring to take place. The linen may also be prepared with a watery extract of aloes, made either hot or cold. Dry ammoniacal vapour does not oxidize aloes. True, the necessary oxygen is in the air, but water helps its action. We experimented with myrrh, but the action was very feeble.

RESEARCHES AS TO NEGATIVE IMPRESSIONS

Eventually we surmounted our difficulties, and obtained a perfectly plain negative image by the following device. We took the plaster cast of a hand and covered it with a glove of suéde kid. We then poured some of the ammoniacal solution along the wrist so that it penetrated the plaster without completely saturating the glove. The vapours were given off very regularly through the pores of the kid without staining the linen by too much water or letting the oil penetrate the damp glove. [1]

Working in this way we got an excellent impression of the back of the hand. The tips of the fingers have the square aspect due to the glove having been too long. On the inside of the thumb the seams of the glove are plainly to be seen, while on the outside the image fades away rapidly and regularly. The print is sufficiently definite to show the likeness of a finger, but too diffuse to mark the actual outlines, and this may be said of all the fingers. On the back of the hand the slight depressions between the metacarpals are easily distinguished, the outer edge going off into an unfinished blot where the linen had been raised above the object by the higher position of the fourth and fifth fingers.

The print which we have obtained of this hand justifies us in asserting that under special conditions ammoniacal vapours may produce as distinct impressions of an object as those shown on the Holy Shroud.

The experiment is so delicate that on a second trial the same glove did not produce so good a print as the first. Having been dried and re-moistened the texture no longer constituted so good a filter.

We tried vainly to make as good a print of a plaster head of Michael Angelo, which seemed to be a good subject. Here the nose did not project much beyond the mouth, and the beard projecting brought the face almost into one plane. But so far we have not succeeded in doing anything with the bare plaster.

We shall continue these experiments if desirable, though they only present a limited interest. It has been proved by the gloved hand that an object in relief will give a negative image when it exhales ammonia-

---

[1] For a reason explained further on, it was not positively with ammoniacal water that we did not moisten the plaster with a solution of ammonia, but with one of ammonium carbonate.

cal vapours on a cloth prepared with a mixture of aloes. Henceforth our problem is to discover under what circumstances *a human body may become itself the source of such active vapours.*

When we consider among substances contained in human economy those which are capable of emitting ammoniacal vapours, the first thing we think of is *urea.* Urea when it ferments is completely transformed into carbonate of ammonia, which in its turn gives out ammoniacal vapours very regularly.[1] Here is the formula of urea and the well known equation which expresses its transformation.

$$N^2 \!\!\begin{array}{c} CO \\ H_4 \end{array} + 2H_2O = {}^2 \begin{array}{c} NH_4 \\ CO \end{array}\!\! O_2$$

urea   carbonate of ammonia

For this reason, when we tried to obtain an impression of a gloved hand, we used carbonate of ammonia, wishing to reproduce the conditions of the natural fermentation of an organic liquid rich in urea.

This is how the problem now presents itself as a physiological study.

Let us take a body coated with a sufficient quantity of urea; this urea will ferment. From this ammoniacal vapours will emanate little by little so long as the urea lasts, vapours which shall be capable of staining linen saturated with oil and aloes and of reproducing the negative impression or image of a body.

We assert that in order to fulfil these conditions naturally it is only necessary that the body shall be covered with pathologic sweat, and specially the sweat of fever.

In normal sweat besides chloride of sodium, there are present mineral salts and certain alkaline salts, with mineral acids, and with these a proportion of urea—only a small quantity, four centigrammes to a litre of sweat according to some authorities, but a rather larger proportion according to others.[2] Funke says that when the sweat increases the quantity of urea

---

[1] We have obtained the particulars which follow from the remarkable *Traité de chimie appliquée à la physiologie,* by M. le Professeur Armand Gautier, membre de l'Académie des Sciences.

[2] "From the figures given above," says M. Gautier, "the excretions in sweat from an adult would be ·4 gr. of urea in twenty-four hours." But according to Funke this excretion would be much more abundant. It would amount to as much as 1 gr. 55 per litre.

and of mineral salts also increases a little, whilst other organic substances decrease.

But the remarkable thing is that *in morbid sweat* the increase of urea is quite astonishing. M. Gautier says : " Urea may be produced so abundantly in certain morbid sweats that it forms crystals on the surface of the body. A fringe of such crystals has been seen on the forehead where it joins the hair, presenting an appearance like down." And again : " It may be stated that in many illnesses the presence of carbonate of ammonia causes the sweat to become abnormally alkaline. . . . It is the opinion of Andral that in fever the normal acidity of the sweat diminishes or even disappears, returning when the fever diminishes. . . . All viscous sweat is neutral or barely acid " (pp. 433, 434).

M. Gautier also personally assured me that viscous sweat strongly charged with urea would be given off by any fever patient in a crisis of pain. Further—and this is of great importance—a man who has been tortured for a length of time will at death be found to have his body covered with a deposit rich in urea. This deposit left after the heavy sweating, caused by acute pain, has somewhat evaporated. The skin would remain moist. If, then, after death such a corpse were covered with a sheet soaked in aloes, the urea would ferment, carbonate of ammonia would be produced, ammoniacal vapours would arise ; these vapours would oxidize the aloes, and would produce on the cloth a negative by chemical action.[1]

We will not at present proceed further with our chemical experiments. We have ascertained that aloes fulfils the two-fold conditions necessary for a substance which could produce such impressions as those found on the Holy Shroud.

It was necessary to find a substance capable of producing impressions which should resemble in appearance those on the cloth at Turin. Aloes gives us these impressions. It was necessary that the chemical action should have a physiological cause, and it is to the emanation of vapour from an organic body that the aloes owe their discoloration.

While keeping within the physical conditions of the experiment made

[1] Edition of 1874, vol. II. p. 81.

THE SHROUD OF CHRIST

with zinc we have yet crossed the limit which divides theory from practice. We attribute the impressions on the Shroud therefore to direct chemical action, spontaneously and even necessarily produced under conditions which can be clearly defined.

We now know what name to give to these impressions, if any one seeks to coin a new word—they are *vaporographic prints*.

LIST OF RECENT PUBLICATIONS CONCERNING THE
HOLY SHROUD OF TURIN

Ulysse Chevalier, *Le Saint Suaire de Turin est il l'original ou une copie?* *Étude critique* Chambéry : V. Ménard, 1899, in 8vo, 31 pages.

Réponse aux observations de Mgr. Emmanuel Colomiatte, provicaire général de Turin, on the pamphlet : *Le Saint Suaire de Turin est il l'original ou une copie ?* Paris : Picard, 1900, in 8vo, 8 pages.

Étude critique sur l'origine du Saint Suaire de Lirey-Chambéry-Turin. Paris : Picard, 1900, in 8vo, 8 pages.

Arthur Loth. *Le portrait de N. S. Jésus Christ d'après le Saint Suaire de Turin.* Paris : Oudin, 1900, in 8vo, 64 pages, 4 plates.

P. G. Sanna Solaro. *La S. Sindone che si venera a Torrino illustrata e difesa.* Torino : Vincenza Bona, in 4to, 179 pages, 20 figures.

www.ingramcontent.com/pod-product-compliance
Lightning Source LLC
Chambersburg PA
CBHW021102090426
42738CB00006B/465